365

DAYS OF

GRATITUDE

JOURNAL

365

DAYS OF GRATITUDE JOURNAL

Commit to the life-changing power of gratitude by creating a sustainable practice

Mariëlle S. Smith

TO SHANE

Introduction

Welcome to *365 Days of Gratitude*, a journal for those who want to create a sustainable gratitude practice. I'm so grateful that you're here.

Over the years, I've tested various ways of 'doing' gratitude journaling, keeping what served me and discarding what didn't. What you have in front of you right now is what I kept after all that trying.

Why gratitude?

I'm not here to sell you on gratitude. There are many articles and research papers I could be citing to convince you just how great practising gratitude is for you. I think you're already aware of that, though. Perhaps you've read some of those articles and papers or maybe you just know it somewhere deep down —or not so deep down.

I'm not hooked on gratitude because it works wonders on my blood pressure and promises to help me sleep better. Although it probably does that, too.

I'm hooked on gratitude because it enables me to perceive everything in life as magical again. I'm hooked because I'm not the same person I was since I started practising it. And because I slip and return to being that anxious, burned out, overachieving workaholic as soon as I stray from the gratitude path—which happens far more often than I care to admit.

Gratitude is a commitment for life. I created this journal to help you commit and turn your gratitude practice into a sustainable one.

Serendipity + structure = sustainability

Serendipity

My gratitude practice started almost three years ago. I had a job that drained me, was in a relationship that hadn't been working for quite some time, and my yoga practice didn't fulfil me the way it used to. I had picked up regular journaling a few months prior and—hoping it would help snap me out of whatever I was going through at the time—had also committed myself to a daily meditation practice.

About a week after I started my daily meditations, I ran into an old university buddy from the time I lived in Dublin. Over the years, my once cynical friend had developed a dedicated daily meditation and gratitude practice.

I had dabbled in gratitude journaling before but had never been able to stick with it. I thought it wasn't for me. Then again, I couldn't quite believe just how much my friend had changed since we met last... When he offered to share the prompts he used in his daily gratitude practice before we went our separate ways, I didn't hesitate.

Structure

During my original attempts at gratitude journaling, I simply tried to write down at least one thing that had made me grateful that day. For whatever reason, that didn't work for me. Those prompts my friend shared did work.

Now that I had specific questions to answer, writing down what I felt grateful for no longer felt forced. I wasn't staring at the page anymore, trying to figure out what to write about. It made it so much easier to return the next day, and the next. It also enabled me to compare my answers and track my progress, which kept me coming back for more.

Once I realised which of the prompts didn't work for me, I began to leave some out, modified others, and brought in new questions to answer, the final result of which I am now sharing with you.

Sustainability

Gratitude journaling brings me so much. It slows me down. It reminds me to take deep breaths in and out. It stops me from pushing myself too hard, too often. It brings me joy. Happiness. Appreciation. It reminds me of all I have going for me, no matter the kind of day it's been.

It really has been the key I was looking and ready for when it showed up in my life.

But, even now, after years of practice, I have to consciously decide to do the work. That it came at the right time and with the structure I needed doesn't mean I don't get off track, especially when the going gets tough.

I used to become angry and utterly frustrated with myself when this happened, but now I simply sit myself down (read: force myself to take a break) and return to my practice. And because it's such a simple, structured practice, it's easier to pick up again than I often think.

Of course, some days or even weeks will be easier than others, but that's another thing gratitude journaling has brought me. No matter how far I stray, I am grateful for having something to return to. For all the days I ignore my practice, I'm grateful for all the days I do pick up my journal and let the miracle that is life unfold in front of me.

That attitude, that's what gratitude practice is all about for me. And I would never have developed it if it weren't for the prompts in this book. It is my hope that they will help you develop that same attitude so you can reap the same benefits.

Mariëlle

How to use 365 Days of Gratitude

This undated journal is set up as an evening journal, something you attend to when leaving the day behind. However, if you prefer to do your gratitude practice in the morning, just answer the prompts about the previous day instead. (I do so all the time.)

- Daily prompts

Three things I'm grateful for

Here, you get to write down the things you're grateful for, whether they are general or specific to that day. You can also mix it up and, for example, write down one thing you're grateful for in general and two things you're grateful for that happened in the past twenty-four hours.

I give today a

I rate my days anywhere between 1 and 10, but you might be more comfortable using a star system or rating your days from 1 to 5.

Something I want to remember about today

Anything in particular you want to remember about that day goes here. This could be anything, whether big or small.

Something I could have been more grateful for today

Here, you get to ponder something you could have been more grateful for that day. Perhaps something happened that you weren't grateful for at the time. Or maybe you took something for granted that you wish you hadn't. Whatever it is, here you get the chance to express gratitude for it after all.

My intention for tomorrow

No matter how the day went, there's always the next. Here, you can write down your intention for that next day. With what mindset do you want to tackle it? With what attitude towards yourself and others?

- Weekly & four-weekly prompts

Most weekly and four-weekly prompts are almost identical to the daily ones. However, instead of asking you to reflect on one day, you're asked to think back on the past week or four-week period as a whole.

Someone I could have felt more grateful for

Similar to the *Something I could have felt more grateful for* prompt, this prompt invites you to think of an individual, or individuals, who you could have been more grateful for. Did you have any encounters or conversations over the past week or four-week period that, in hindsight, you could have appreciated more?

Perhaps someone said 'No' to something and it turned out a big or small blessing. Maybe you had trouble feeling grateful for someone else's happiness or success. Whatever it was, here you get the chance to express gratitude for it after all.

- Quarterly prompts

Next to the ones you're already familiar with, the three-month checkpoint also includes prompts that invite you to pause a little longer and reflect a little deeper.

Looking back over the past three months, I am most grateful for

Here, I invite you to leaf through the past quarter. What do you notice about your previous entries and what, when looking back, are you the most grateful for?

The biggest lesson I learned over the past three months

What bigger lessons do your previous entries point towards? How can these be summed up best?

When looking back on how I've rated my weeks thus far, the numbers tell me

When comparing how you've rated the previous weeks, have you been doing better than you thought? Worse? Or have you been doing exactly like you thought you were? Have you been honest with your ratings or have you been pushing it? Whatever comes up, write it down.

What/who have I been unable to feel grateful for during the past three months?

No matter how much gratitude you have practised over the past quarter, there might still be that one (or more) thing, event, person that you just haven't been able to feel any gratitude towards.

Here, I invite you to rephrase your thoughts anyway, even if you're not feeling it (yet). Writing it down might just shift something for you, even if it's minor. You don't have to start with your biggest struggle here. If this is particularly hard for you, pick whatever feels doable.

I've said it before, but I will say it again: practising gratitude truly is a commitment for life. I hope that the prompts discussed here will help you turn your practice into a habit you can't help but return to.

THE STRUGGLE ENDS
WHEN GRATITUDE BEGINS.

Neale Donald Walsch

DAY   MONTH   YEAR

THREE THINGS I'M GRATEFUL FOR

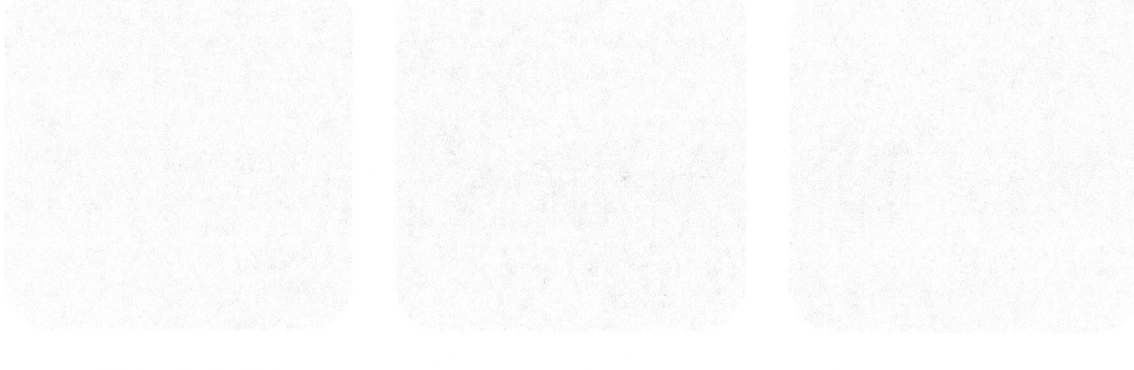

I GIVE TODAY A

SOMETHING I WANT TO REMEMBER ABOUT TODAY

SOMETHING I COULD HAVE BEEN MORE GRATEFUL FOR TODAY

MY INTENTION FOR TOMORROW

DAY 2

DAY   MONTH   YEAR

THREE THINGS I'M GRATEFUL FOR

SOMETHING I WANT TO REMEMBER ABOUT TODAY

I GIVE TODAY A

MY INTENTION FOR TOMORROW

SOMETHING I COULD HAVE BEEN MORE GRATEFUL FOR TODAY

DAY 3

DAY   MONTH   YEAR

THREE THINGS I'M GRATEFUL FOR

I GIVE TODAY A

SOMETHING I WANT TO REMEMBER ABOUT TODAY

SOMETHING I COULD HAVE BEEN MORE GRATEFUL FOR TODAY

MY INTENTION FOR TOMORROW

DAY 4

THREE THINGS I'M GRATEFUL FOR

SOMETHING I WANT TO REMEMBER ABOUT TODAY

I GIVE TODAY A

MY INTENTION FOR TOMORROW

SOMETHING I COULD HAVE BEEN MORE GRATEFUL FOR TODAY

DAY 5

DAY   MONTH   YEAR

THREE THINGS I'M GRATEFUL FOR

I GIVE TODAY A

SOMETHING I WANT TO REMEMBER ABOUT TODAY

SOMETHING I COULD HAVE BEEN MORE GRATEFUL FOR TODAY

MY INTENTION FOR TOMORROW

DAY 6

DAY   MONTH   YEAR

THREE THINGS I'M GRATEFUL FOR

SOMETHING I WANT TO REMEMBER ABOUT TODAY

I GIVE TODAY A

MY INTENTION FOR
TOMORROW

SOMETHING I COULD HAVE BEEN MORE GRATEFUL FOR TODAY

DAY 7

DAY   MONTH   YEAR

THREE THINGS I'M GRATEFUL FOR

I GIVE TODAY A

SOMETHING I WANT TO REMEMBER ABOUT TODAY

SOMETHING I COULD HAVE BEEN MORE GRATEFUL FOR TODAY

MY INTENTION FOR TOMORROW

DAY 7

WE'RE ALL SO BUSY CHASING THE EXTRAORDINARY THAT
WE FORGET TO STOP AND BE GRATEFUL FOR THE ORDINARY.

BRENÉ BROWN

SOMETHING I COULD HAVE BEEN MORE GRATEFUL FOR THIS WEEK

I GIVE THIS WEEK A

SOMETHING I WANT TO REMEMBER ABOUT THIS WEEK

MY INTENTION FOR NEXT
WEEK

SOMEONE I COULD HAVE FELT MORE GRATEFUL FOR THIS WEEK

DAY 8

DAY   MONTH   YEAR

THREE THINGS I'M GRATEFUL FOR

I GIVE TODAY A

SOMETHING I WANT TO REMEMBER ABOUT TODAY

SOMETHING I COULD HAVE BEEN MORE GRATEFUL FOR TODAY

MY INTENTION FOR TOMORROW

DAY 9

THREE THINGS I'M GRATEFUL FOR

SOMETHING I WANT TO REMEMBER ABOUT TODAY

I GIVE TODAY A

MY INTENTION FOR
TOMORROW

SOMETHING I COULD HAVE BEEN MORE GRATEFUL FOR TODAY

DAY 10

DAY   MONTH   YEAR

THREE THINGS I'M GRATEFUL FOR

I GIVE TODAY A

SOMETHING I WANT TO REMEMBER ABOUT TODAY

SOMETHING I COULD HAVE BEEN MORE GRATEFUL FOR TODAY

MY INTENTION FOR
TOMORROW

DAY 11

THREE THINGS I'M GRATEFUL FOR

SOMETHING I WANT TO REMEMBER ABOUT TODAY

I GIVE TODAY A

MY INTENTION FOR
TOMORROW

SOMETHING I COULD HAVE BEEN MORE GRATEFUL FOR TODAY

DAY 12

DAY   MONTH   YEAR

THREE THINGS I'M GRATEFUL FOR

I GIVE TODAY A

SOMETHING I WANT TO REMEMBER ABOUT TODAY

SOMETHING I COULD HAVE BEEN MORE GRATEFUL FOR TODAY

MY INTENTION FOR TOMORROW

DAY 13

THREE THINGS I'M GRATEFUL FOR

SOMETHING I WANT TO REMEMBER ABOUT TODAY

I GIVE TODAY A

MY INTENTION FOR
TOMORROW

SOMETHING I COULD HAVE BEEN MORE GRATEFUL FOR TODAY

DAY 14

DAY   MONTH   YEAR

THREE THINGS I'M GRATEFUL FOR

I GIVE TODAY A

SOMETHING I WANT TO REMEMBER ABOUT TODAY

SOMETHING I COULD HAVE BEEN MORE GRATEFUL FOR TODAY

MY INTENTION FOR TOMORROW

DAY 14

IT IS NOT JOY THAT MAKES US GRATEFUL, IT IS
GRATITUDE THAT MAKES US JOYFUL.

DAVID STEINDL-RAST

SOMETHING I COULD HAVE BEEN MORE GRATEFUL FOR THIS WEEK

I GIVE THIS WEEK A

SOMETHING I WANT TO REMEMBER ABOUT THIS WEEK

MY INTENTION FOR NEXT
WEEK

SOMEONE I COULD HAVE FELT MORE GRATEFUL FOR THIS WEEK

DAY 15

DAY	MONTH	YEAR

THREE THINGS I'M GRATEFUL FOR

I GIVE TODAY A

SOMETHING I WANT TO REMEMBER ABOUT TODAY

SOMETHING I COULD HAVE BEEN MORE GRATEFUL FOR TODAY

MY INTENTION FOR TOMORROW

DAY 16

THREE THINGS I'M GRATEFUL FOR

SOMETHING I WANT TO REMEMBER ABOUT TODAY

I GIVE TODAY A

MY INTENTION FOR
TOMORROW

SOMETHING I COULD HAVE BEEN MORE GRATEFUL FOR TODAY

DAY 17

DAY   MONTH   YEAR

THREE THINGS I'M GRATEFUL FOR

I GIVE TODAY A

SOMETHING I WANT TO REMEMBER ABOUT TODAY

SOMETHING I COULD HAVE BEEN MORE GRATEFUL FOR TODAY

MY INTENTION FOR TOMORROW

DAY MONTH YEAR

THREE THINGS I'M GRATEFUL FOR

SOMETHING I WANT TO REMEMBER ABOUT TODAY I GIVE TODAY A

MY INTENTION FOR
TOMORROW SOMETHING I COULD HAVE BEEN MORE GRATEFUL FOR TODAY

DAY 19

DAY   MONTH   YEAR

THREE THINGS I'M GRATEFUL FOR

I GIVE TODAY A

SOMETHING I WANT TO REMEMBER ABOUT TODAY

SOMETHING I COULD HAVE BEEN MORE GRATEFUL FOR TODAY

MY INTENTION FOR
TOMORROW

DAY   MONTH   YEAR

THREE THINGS I'M GRATEFUL FOR

SOMETHING I WANT TO REMEMBER ABOUT TODAY   I GIVE TODAY A

MY INTENTION FOR
TOMORROW   SOMETHING I COULD HAVE BEEN MORE GRATEFUL FOR TODAY

DAY 21

DAY MONTH YEAR

THREE THINGS I'M GRATEFUL FOR

I GIVE TODAY A

SOMETHING I WANT TO REMEMBER ABOUT TODAY

SOMETHING I COULD HAVE BEEN MORE GRATEFUL FOR TODAY

MY INTENTION FOR TOMORROW

EXPECT NOTHING. APPRECIATE EVERYTHING.

UNKNOWN

SOMETHING I COULD HAVE BEEN MORE GRATEFUL FOR THIS WEEK

I GIVE THIS WEEK A

SOMETHING I WANT TO REMEMBER ABOUT THIS WEEK

MY INTENTION FOR NEXT WEEK

SOMEONE I COULD HAVE FELT MORE GRATEFUL FOR THIS WEEK

DAY 22

DAY   MONTH   YEAR

THREE THINGS I'M GRATEFUL FOR

I GIVE TODAY A

SOMETHING I WANT TO REMEMBER ABOUT TODAY

SOMETHING I COULD HAVE BEEN MORE GRATEFUL FOR TODAY

MY INTENTION FOR TOMORROW

DAY   MONTH   YEAR

THREE THINGS I'M GRATEFUL FOR

SOMETHING I WANT TO REMEMBER ABOUT TODAY

I GIVE TODAY A

MY INTENTION FOR
TOMORROW

SOMETHING I COULD HAVE BEEN MORE GRATEFUL FOR TODAY

# DAY 24

DAY   MONTH   YEAR

THREE THINGS I'M GRATEFUL FOR

I GIVE TODAY A

SOMETHING I WANT TO REMEMBER ABOUT TODAY

SOMETHING I COULD HAVE BEEN MORE GRATEFUL FOR TODAY

MY INTENTION FOR
TOMORROW

DAY 25

THREE THINGS I'M GRATEFUL FOR

SOMETHING I WANT TO REMEMBER ABOUT TODAY

I GIVE TODAY A

MY INTENTION FOR
TOMORROW

SOMETHING I COULD HAVE BEEN MORE GRATEFUL FOR TODAY

DAY 26

DAY   MONTH   YEAR

THREE THINGS I'M GRATEFUL FOR

I GIVE TODAY A

SOMETHING I WANT TO REMEMBER ABOUT TODAY

SOMETHING I COULD HAVE BEEN MORE GRATEFUL FOR TODAY

MY INTENTION FOR TOMORROW

 # DAY 27 

DAY   MONTH   YEAR

THREE THINGS I'M GRATEFUL FOR

SOMETHING I WANT TO REMEMBER ABOUT TODAY

I GIVE TODAY A

MY INTENTION FOR
TOMORROW

SOMETHING I COULD HAVE BEEN MORE GRATEFUL FOR TODAY

DAY 28

Day	Month	Year

Three things I'm grateful for

I give today a

Something I want to remember about today

Something I could have been more grateful for today

My intention for tomorrow

DAY 28

WK 4

GRATITUDE UNLOCKS THE FULLNESS OF LIFE. IT TURNS WHAT WE HAVE INTO ENOUGH, AND MORE. IT TURNS DENIAL INTO ACCEPTANCE, CHAOS TO ORDER, CONFUSION TO CLARITY. IT CAN TURN A MEAL INTO A FEAST, A HOUSE INTO A HOME, A STRANGER INTO A FRIEND. GRATITUDE MAKES SENSE OF OUR PAST, BRINGS PEACE FOR TODAY AND CREATES A VISION FOR TOMORROW.
MELODY BEATTIE

SOMETHING I COULD HAVE BEEN MORE GRATEFUL FOR THESE PAST FOUR WEEKS

I GIVE THE PAST FOUR WEEKS A

SOMETHING I WANT TO REMEMBER ABOUT THE PAST FOUR WEEKS

MY INTENTION FOR THE NEXT FOUR WEEKS

SOMEONE I COULD HAVE FELT MORE GRATEFUL FOR THESE PAST FOUR WEEKS

DAY 29

DAY   MONTH   YEAR

THREE THINGS I'M GRATEFUL FOR

I GIVE TODAY A

SOMETHING I WANT TO REMEMBER ABOUT TODAY

SOMETHING I COULD HAVE BEEN MORE GRATEFUL FOR TODAY

MY INTENTION FOR TOMORROW

DAY 30

THREE THINGS I'M GRATEFUL FOR

SOMETHING I WANT TO REMEMBER ABOUT TODAY

I GIVE TODAY A

MY INTENTION FOR TOMORROW

SOMETHING I COULD HAVE BEEN MORE GRATEFUL FOR TODAY

DAY 31

THREE THINGS I'M GRATEFUL FOR

I GIVE TODAY A

SOMETHING I WANT TO REMEMBER ABOUT TODAY

SOMETHING I COULD HAVE BEEN MORE GRATEFUL FOR TODAY

MY INTENTION FOR
TOMORROW

DAY 32

THREE THINGS I'M GRATEFUL FOR

SOMETHING I WANT TO REMEMBER ABOUT TODAY

I GIVE TODAY A

MY INTENTION FOR
TOMORROW

SOMETHING I COULD HAVE BEEN MORE GRATEFUL FOR TODAY

DAY 33

DAY   MONTH   YEAR

THREE THINGS I'M GRATEFUL FOR

I GIVE TODAY A

SOMETHING I WANT TO REMEMBER ABOUT TODAY

SOMETHING I COULD HAVE BEEN MORE GRATEFUL FOR TODAY

MY INTENTION FOR TOMORROW

DAY   MONTH   YEAR

THREE THINGS I'M GRATEFUL FOR

SOMETHING I WANT TO REMEMBER ABOUT TODAY

I GIVE TODAY A

MY INTENTION FOR
TOMORROW

SOMETHING I COULD HAVE BEEN MORE GRATEFUL FOR TODAY

DAY 35

DAY   MONTH   YEAR

THREE THINGS I'M GRATEFUL FOR

I GIVE TODAY A

SOMETHING I WANT TO REMEMBER ABOUT TODAY

SOMETHING I COULD HAVE BEEN MORE GRATEFUL FOR TODAY

MY INTENTION FOR
TOMORROW

DAY 35

EVERY DAY MAY NOT BE GOOD… BUT THERE'S SOMETHING GOOD IN EVERY DAY.

Alice Morse Earle

SOMETHING I COULD HAVE BEEN MORE GRATEFUL FOR THIS WEEK

I GIVE THIS WEEK A

SOMETHING I WANT TO REMEMBER ABOUT THIS WEEK

MY INTENTION FOR NEXT WEEK

SOMEONE I COULD HAVE FELT MORE GRATEFUL FOR THIS WEEK

DAY 36

DAY   MONTH   YEAR

THREE THINGS I'M GRATEFUL FOR

I GIVE TODAY A

SOMETHING I WANT TO REMEMBER ABOUT TODAY

SOMETHING I COULD HAVE BEEN MORE GRATEFUL FOR TODAY

MY INTENTION FOR
TOMORROW

DAY 37

THREE THINGS I'M GRATEFUL FOR

SOMETHING I WANT TO REMEMBER ABOUT TODAY

I GIVE TODAY A

MY INTENTION FOR TOMORROW

SOMETHING I COULD HAVE BEEN MORE GRATEFUL FOR TODAY

DAY 38

Day   Month   Year

Three things I'm grateful for

I GIVE TODAY A

SOMETHING I WANT TO REMEMBER ABOUT TODAY

SOMETHING I COULD HAVE BEEN MORE GRATEFUL FOR TODAY

MY INTENTION FOR
TOMORROW

DAY 39

DAY   MONTH   YEAR

THREE THINGS I'M GRATEFUL FOR

SOMETHING I WANT TO REMEMBER ABOUT TODAY

I GIVE TODAY A

MY INTENTION FOR
TOMORROW

SOMETHING I COULD HAVE BEEN MORE GRATEFUL FOR TODAY

DAY   MONTH   YEAR

THREE THINGS I'M GRATEFUL FOR

I GIVE TODAY A

SOMETHING I WANT TO REMEMBER ABOUT TODAY

SOMETHING I COULD HAVE BEEN MORE GRATEFUL FOR TODAY

MY INTENTION FOR
TOMORROW

DAY 41

Day   Month   Year

Three things I'm grateful for

Something I want to remember about today

I give today a

My intention for
tomorrow

Something I could have been more grateful for today

DAY 42

DAY   MONTH   YEAR

THREE THINGS I'M GRATEFUL FOR

I GIVE TODAY A

SOMETHING I WANT TO REMEMBER ABOUT TODAY

SOMETHING I COULD HAVE BEEN MORE GRATEFUL FOR TODAY

MY INTENTION FOR
TOMORROW

DAY 42

THE REAL GIFT OF GRATITUDE IS THAT THE MORE
GRATEFUL YOU ARE, THE MORE PRESENT YOU BECOME.

ROBERT HOLDEN

SOMETHING I COULD HAVE BEEN MORE GRATEFUL FOR THIS WEEK

I GIVE THIS WEEK A

SOMETHING I WANT TO REMEMBER ABOUT THIS WEEK

MY INTENTION FOR NEXT
WEEK

SOMEONE I COULD HAVE FELT MORE GRATEFUL FOR THIS WEEK

DAY MONTH YEAR

THREE THINGS I'M GRATEFUL FOR

I GIVE TODAY A

SOMETHING I WANT TO REMEMBER ABOUT TODAY

SOMETHING I COULD HAVE BEEN MORE GRATEFUL FOR TODAY

MY INTENTION FOR TOMORROW

DAY 44

THREE THINGS I'M GRATEFUL FOR

SOMETHING I WANT TO REMEMBER ABOUT TODAY

I GIVE TODAY A

MY INTENTION FOR
TOMORROW

SOMETHING I COULD HAVE BEEN MORE GRATEFUL FOR TODAY

DAY   MONTH   YEAR

THREE THINGS I'M GRATEFUL FOR

I GIVE TODAY A

SOMETHING I WANT TO REMEMBER ABOUT TODAY

SOMETHING I COULD HAVE BEEN MORE GRATEFUL FOR TODAY

MY INTENTION FOR
TOMORROW

DAY   MONTH   YEAR

THREE THINGS I'M GRATEFUL FOR

SOMETHING I WANT TO REMEMBER ABOUT TODAY   I GIVE TODAY A

MY INTENTION FOR   SOMETHING I COULD HAVE BEEN MORE GRATEFUL FOR TODAY
TOMORROW

DAY 47

DAY   MONTH   YEAR

THREE THINGS I'M GRATEFUL FOR

I GIVE TODAY A

SOMETHING I WANT TO REMEMBER ABOUT TODAY

SOMETHING I COULD HAVE BEEN MORE GRATEFUL FOR TODAY

MY INTENTION FOR TOMORROW

THREE THINGS I'M GRATEFUL FOR

SOMETHING I WANT TO REMEMBER ABOUT TODAY

I GIVE TODAY A

MY INTENTION FOR
TOMORROW

SOMETHING I COULD HAVE BEEN MORE GRATEFUL FOR TODAY

DAY   MONTH   YEAR

THREE THINGS I'M GRATEFUL FOR

I GIVE TODAY A

SOMETHING I WANT TO REMEMBER ABOUT TODAY

SOMETHING I COULD HAVE BEEN MORE GRATEFUL FOR TODAY

MY INTENTION FOR
TOMORROW

DAY 49

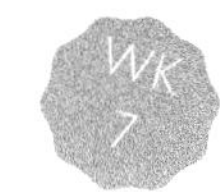

At the end of the day, I am thankful that my blessings are bigger than my problems.

UNKNOWN

SOMETHING I COULD HAVE BEEN MORE GRATEFUL FOR THIS WEEK

I GIVE THIS WEEK A

SOMETHING I WANT TO REMEMBER ABOUT THIS WEEK

MY INTENTION FOR NEXT WEEK

SOMEONE I COULD HAVE FELT MORE GRATEFUL FOR THIS WEEK

DAY   MONTH   YEAR

THREE THINGS I'M GRATEFUL FOR

I GIVE TODAY A

SOMETHING I WANT TO REMEMBER ABOUT TODAY

SOMETHING I COULD HAVE BEEN MORE GRATEFUL FOR TODAY

MY INTENTION FOR TOMORROW

DAY 51

DAY   MONTH   YEAR

THREE THINGS I'M GRATEFUL FOR

SOMETHING I WANT TO REMEMBER ABOUT TODAY

I GIVE TODAY A

MY INTENTION FOR TOMORROW

SOMETHING I COULD HAVE BEEN MORE GRATEFUL FOR TODAY

DAY 52

DAY   MONTH   YEAR

THREE THINGS I'M GRATEFUL FOR

I GIVE TODAY A

SOMETHING I WANT TO REMEMBER ABOUT TODAY

SOMETHING I COULD HAVE BEEN MORE GRATEFUL FOR TODAY

MY INTENTION FOR
TOMORROW

DAY 53

Day   Month   Year

Three things I'm grateful for

Something I want to remember about today

I give today a

My intention for
tomorrow

Something I could have been more grateful for today

DAY 54

DAY   MONTH   YEAR

THREE THINGS I'M GRATEFUL FOR

I GIVE TODAY A

SOMETHING I WANT TO REMEMBER ABOUT TODAY

SOMETHING I COULD HAVE BEEN MORE GRATEFUL FOR TODAY

MY INTENTION FOR
TOMORROW

DAY 55

THREE THINGS I'M GRATEFUL FOR

SOMETHING I WANT TO REMEMBER ABOUT TODAY

I GIVE TODAY A

MY INTENTION FOR
TOMORROW

SOMETHING I COULD HAVE BEEN MORE GRATEFUL FOR TODAY

DAY 56

DAY　　　MONTH　　　YEAR

THREE THINGS I'M GRATEFUL FOR

I GIVE TODAY A

SOMETHING I WANT TO REMEMBER ABOUT TODAY

SOMETHING I COULD HAVE BEEN MORE GRATEFUL FOR TODAY

MY INTENTION FOR TOMORROW

DAY 56

Somebody didn't wake up today, but you did. That's enough reason to stop complaining, and that's enough to be thankful for. Never let your troubles blind you to your daily blessings.

Trent Shelton

Something I could have been more grateful for these past four weeks

I give the past four weeks a

Something I want to remember about the past four weeks

My intention for the next four weeks

Someone I could have felt more grateful for these past four weeks

DAY 57

THREE THINGS I'M GRATEFUL FOR

I GIVE TODAY A

SOMETHING I WANT TO REMEMBER ABOUT TODAY

SOMETHING I COULD HAVE BEEN MORE GRATEFUL FOR TODAY

MY INTENTION FOR
TOMORROW

DAY 58

DAY   MONTH   YEAR

THREE THINGS I'M GRATEFUL FOR

SOMETHING I WANT TO REMEMBER ABOUT TODAY

I GIVE TODAY A

MY INTENTION FOR TOMORROW

SOMETHING I COULD HAVE BEEN MORE GRATEFUL FOR TODAY

DAY 59

DAY   MONTH   YEAR

THREE THINGS I'M GRATEFUL FOR

I GIVE TODAY A

SOMETHING I WANT TO REMEMBER ABOUT TODAY

SOMETHING I COULD HAVE BEEN MORE GRATEFUL FOR TODAY

MY INTENTION FOR TOMORROW

DAY 60

DAY   MONTH   YEAR

THREE THINGS I'M GRATEFUL FOR

SOMETHING I WANT TO REMEMBER ABOUT TODAY   I GIVE TODAY A

MY INTENTION FOR TOMORROW   SOMETHING I COULD HAVE BEEN MORE GRATEFUL FOR TODAY

DAY 61

DAY   MONTH   YEAR

THREE THINGS I'M GRATEFUL FOR

I GIVE TODAY A

SOMETHING I WANT TO REMEMBER ABOUT TODAY

SOMETHING I COULD HAVE BEEN MORE GRATEFUL FOR TODAY

MY INTENTION FOR TOMORROW

Day 62

Day   Month   Year

Three things I'm grateful for

Something I want to remember about today

I give today a

My intention for
tomorrow

Something I could have been more grateful for today

DAY 63

THREE THINGS I'M GRATEFUL FOR

I GIVE TODAY A

SOMETHING I WANT TO REMEMBER ABOUT TODAY

SOMETHING I COULD HAVE BEEN MORE GRATEFUL FOR TODAY

MY INTENTION FOR
TOMORROW

DAY 63

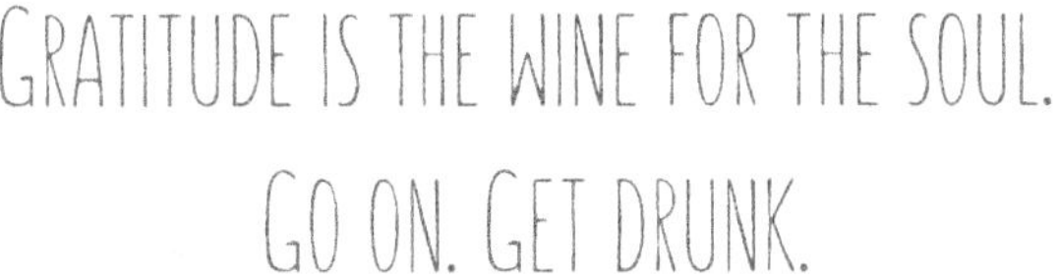

GRATITUDE IS THE WINE FOR THE SOUL.
GO ON. GET DRUNK.

RUMI

SOMETHING I COULD HAVE BEEN MORE GRATEFUL FOR THIS WEEK

I GIVE THIS WEEK A

SOMETHING I WANT TO REMEMBER ABOUT THIS WEEK

MY INTENTION FOR NEXT WEEK

SOMEONE I COULD HAVE FELT MORE GRATEFUL FOR THIS WEEK

DAY 64

DAY   MONTH   YEAR

THREE THINGS I'M GRATEFUL FOR

I GIVE TODAY A

SOMETHING I WANT TO REMEMBER ABOUT TODAY

SOMETHING I COULD HAVE BEEN MORE GRATEFUL FOR TODAY

MY INTENTION FOR TOMORROW

DAY 65

THREE THINGS I'M GRATEFUL FOR

SOMETHING I WANT TO REMEMBER ABOUT TODAY

I GIVE TODAY A

MY INTENTION FOR
TOMORROW

SOMETHING I COULD HAVE BEEN MORE GRATEFUL FOR TODAY

DAY 66

DAY   MONTH   YEAR

THREE THINGS I'M GRATEFUL FOR

I GIVE TODAY A

SOMETHING I WANT TO REMEMBER ABOUT TODAY

SOMETHING I COULD HAVE BEEN MORE GRATEFUL FOR TODAY

MY INTENTION FOR
TOMORROW

Day   Month   Year

Three things I'm grateful for

Something I want to remember about today   I give today a

My intention for tomorrow   Something I could have been more grateful for today

DAY 68

DAY   MONTH   YEAR

THREE THINGS I'M GRATEFUL FOR

I GIVE TODAY A

SOMETHING I WANT TO REMEMBER ABOUT TODAY

SOMETHING I COULD HAVE BEEN MORE GRATEFUL FOR TODAY

MY INTENTION FOR
TOMORROW

DAY 69

THREE THINGS I'M GRATEFUL FOR

SOMETHING I WANT TO REMEMBER ABOUT TODAY

I GIVE TODAY A

MY INTENTION FOR
TOMORROW

SOMETHING I COULD HAVE BEEN MORE GRATEFUL FOR TODAY

DAY 70

DAY   MONTH   YEAR

THREE THINGS I'M GRATEFUL FOR

I GIVE TODAY A

SOMETHING I WANT TO REMEMBER ABOUT TODAY

SOMETHING I COULD HAVE BEEN MORE GRATEFUL FOR TODAY

MY INTENTION FOR TOMORROW

FEELING GRATITUDE AND NOT EXPRESSING IT IS LIKE WRAPPING A PRESENT AND NOT GIVING IT.

WILLIAM ARTHUR WARD

SOMETHING I COULD HAVE BEEN MORE GRATEFUL FOR THIS WEEK

I GIVE THIS WEEK A

SOMETHING I WANT TO REMEMBER ABOUT THIS WEEK

MY INTENTION FOR NEXT WEEK

SOMEONE I COULD HAVE FELT MORE GRATEFUL FOR THIS WEEK

DAY   MONTH   YEAR

THREE THINGS I'M GRATEFUL FOR

I GIVE TODAY A

SOMETHING I WANT TO REMEMBER ABOUT TODAY

SOMETHING I COULD HAVE BEEN MORE GRATEFUL FOR TODAY

MY INTENTION FOR
TOMORROW

DAY   MONTH   YEAR

THREE THINGS I'M GRATEFUL FOR

SOMETHING I WANT TO REMEMBER ABOUT TODAY   I GIVE TODAY A

MY INTENTION FOR   SOMETHING I COULD HAVE BEEN MORE GRATEFUL FOR TODAY
TOMORROW

DAY   MONTH   YEAR

THREE THINGS I'M GRATEFUL FOR

I GIVE TODAY A

SOMETHING I WANT TO REMEMBER ABOUT TODAY

SOMETHING I COULD HAVE BEEN MORE GRATEFUL FOR TODAY

MY INTENTION FOR
TOMORROW

Day   Month   Year

Three things I'm grateful for

Something I want to remember about today   I give today a

My intention for
tomorrow   Something I could have been more grateful for today

DAY 75

THREE THINGS I'M GRATEFUL FOR

I GIVE TODAY A

SOMETHING I WANT TO REMEMBER ABOUT TODAY

SOMETHING I COULD HAVE BEEN MORE GRATEFUL FOR TODAY

MY INTENTION FOR
TOMORROW

DAY 76

THREE THINGS I'M GRATEFUL FOR

SOMETHING I WANT TO REMEMBER ABOUT TODAY

I GIVE TODAY A

MY INTENTION FOR
TOMORROW

SOMETHING I COULD HAVE BEEN MORE GRATEFUL FOR TODAY

DAY 77

DAY   MONTH   YEAR

THREE THINGS I'M GRATEFUL FOR

I GIVE TODAY A

SOMETHING I WANT TO REMEMBER ABOUT TODAY

SOMETHING I COULD HAVE BEEN MORE GRATEFUL FOR TODAY

MY INTENTION FOR
TOMORROW

DAY 77

WHEN YOU ARE GRATEFUL, AN INVISIBLE BLANKET OF PEACE COVERS YOU, IT MAKES YOU GLOW, IT MAKES YOU HAPPY, STRONG, WARM. GRATITUDE PUTS THE MIND AT EASE ABOUT EVERYTHING AROUND.

OM SWAMI

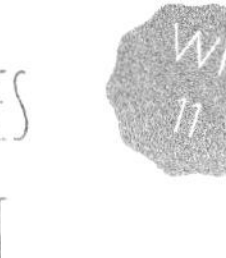

SOMETHING I COULD HAVE BEEN MORE GRATEFUL FOR THIS WEEK

I GIVE THIS WEEK A

SOMETHING I WANT TO REMEMBER ABOUT THIS WEEK

MY INTENTION FOR NEXT WEEK

SOMEONE I COULD HAVE FELT MORE GRATEFUL FOR THIS WEEK

DAY 78

DAY   MONTH   YEAR

THREE THINGS I'M GRATEFUL FOR

I GIVE TODAY A

SOMETHING I WANT TO REMEMBER ABOUT TODAY

SOMETHING I COULD HAVE BEEN MORE GRATEFUL FOR TODAY

MY INTENTION FOR
TOMORROW

DAY 79

THREE THINGS I'M GRATEFUL FOR

SOMETHING I WANT TO REMEMBER ABOUT TODAY

I GIVE TODAY A

MY INTENTION FOR
TOMORROW

SOMETHING I COULD HAVE BEEN MORE GRATEFUL FOR TODAY

DAY 80

DAY	MONTH	YEAR

THREE THINGS I'M GRATEFUL FOR

I GIVE TODAY A

SOMETHING I WANT TO REMEMBER ABOUT TODAY

SOMETHING I COULD HAVE BEEN MORE GRATEFUL FOR TODAY

MY INTENTION FOR TOMORROW

DAY 81

DAY MONTH YEAR

THREE THINGS I'M GRATEFUL FOR

SOMETHING I WANT TO REMEMBER ABOUT TODAY

I GIVE TODAY A

MY INTENTION FOR
TOMORROW

SOMETHING I COULD HAVE BEEN MORE GRATEFUL FOR TODAY

DAY 82

DAY   MONTH   YEAR

THREE THINGS I'M GRATEFUL FOR

I GIVE TODAY A

SOMETHING I WANT TO REMEMBER ABOUT TODAY

SOMETHING I COULD HAVE BEEN MORE GRATEFUL FOR TODAY

MY INTENTION FOR TOMORROW

DAY 83

Day   Month   Year

Three things I'm grateful for

Something I want to remember about today

I give today a

My intention for tomorrow

Something I could have been more grateful for today

DAY 84

DAY   MONTH   YEAR

THREE THINGS I'M GRATEFUL FOR

I GIVE TODAY A

SOMETHING I WANT TO REMEMBER ABOUT TODAY

SOMETHING I COULD HAVE BEEN MORE GRATEFUL FOR TODAY

MY INTENTION FOR TOMORROW

THE BEST TIME TO BE GRATEFUL IS ALWAYS.

UNKNOWN

SOMETHING I COULD HAVE BEEN MORE GRATEFUL FOR THESE PAST FOUR WEEKS

I GIVE THE PAST FOUR WEEKS A

SOMETHING I WANT TO REMEMBER ABOUT THE PAST FOUR WEEKS

MY INTENTION FOR THE NEXT FOUR WEEKS

SOMEONE I COULD HAVE FELT MORE GRATEFUL FOR THESE PAST FOUR WEEKS

Day 85

DAY   MONTH   YEAR

Three things I'm grateful for

I GIVE TODAY A

SOMETHING I WANT TO REMEMBER ABOUT TODAY

SOMETHING I COULD HAVE BEEN MORE GRATEFUL FOR TODAY

MY INTENTION FOR
TOMORROW

DAY 86

DAY   MONTH   YEAR

THREE THINGS I'M GRATEFUL FOR

SOMETHING I WANT TO REMEMBER ABOUT TODAY

I GIVE TODAY A

MY INTENTION FOR TOMORROW

SOMETHING I COULD HAVE BEEN MORE GRATEFUL FOR TODAY

DAY 87

<table>
<tr><td>DAY</td><td>MONTH</td><td>YEAR</td></tr>
</table>

THREE THINGS I'M GRATEFUL FOR

I GIVE TODAY A

SOMETHING I WANT TO REMEMBER ABOUT TODAY

SOMETHING I COULD HAVE BEEN MORE GRATEFUL FOR TODAY

MY INTENTION FOR
TOMORROW

DAY 88

DAY   MONTH   YEAR

THREE THINGS I'M GRATEFUL FOR

SOMETHING I WANT TO REMEMBER ABOUT TODAY

I GIVE TODAY A

MY INTENTION FOR TOMORROW

SOMETHING I COULD HAVE BEEN MORE GRATEFUL FOR TODAY

DAY 89

DAY   MONTH   YEAR

THREE THINGS I'M GRATEFUL FOR

I GIVE TODAY A

SOMETHING I WANT TO REMEMBER ABOUT TODAY

SOMETHING I COULD HAVE BEEN MORE GRATEFUL FOR TODAY

MY INTENTION FOR
TOMORROW

DAY 90

Three things I'm grateful for

Something I want to remember about today

I give today a

My intention for
tomorrow

Something I could have been more grateful for today

DAY   MONTH   YEAR

THREE THINGS I'M GRATEFUL FOR

I GIVE TODAY A

SOMETHING I WANT TO REMEMBER ABOUT TODAY

SOMETHING I COULD HAVE BEEN MORE GRATEFUL FOR TODAY

MY INTENTION FOR TOMORROW

DAY 91

When you are grateful, fear disappears and
abundance appears.

Tony Robbins

Something I could have been more grateful for this week

I give this week a

Something I want to remember about this week

My intention for next
week

Someone I could have felt more grateful for this week

Now you've come this far, it's time to look back.
Leaf through the past thirteen weeks and answer the following:

SOMETHING I WANT TO REMEMBER ABOUT THE PAST THREE MONTHS

LOOKING BACK OVER THE PAST THREE MONTHS, I AM MOST GRATEFUL FOR

THE BIGGEST LESSON I LEARNED OVER THE PAST THREE MONTHS

SOMEONE OR SOMETHING I COULD HAVE FELT MORE GRATEFUL FOR DURING THE PAST THREE MONTHS

I GIVE THE PAST THREE MONTHS A

WHAT HAVE I BEEN UNABLE TO FEEL GRATEFUL FOR DURING THE PAST THREE MONTHS? CAN I REFORMULATE THAT THOUGHT ANYWAY?

I AM GRATEFUL......

WHEN LOOKING BACK ON HOW I'VE RATED MY WEEKS THUS FAR, THE NUMBERS TELL ME

MY INTENTION FOR THE NEXT THREE MONTHS

WHO HAVE I BEEN UNABLE TO FEEL GRATEFUL FOR DURING THE PAST THREE MONTHS? CAN I REFORMULATE THAT THOUGHT ANYWAY? I AM GRATEFUL......

DAY 92

DAY   MONTH   YEAR

THREE THINGS I'M GRATEFUL FOR

I GIVE TODAY A

SOMETHING I WANT TO REMEMBER ABOUT TODAY

SOMETHING I COULD HAVE BEEN MORE GRATEFUL FOR TODAY

MY INTENTION FOR
TOMORROW

DAY 93

THREE THINGS I'M GRATEFUL FOR

SOMETHING I WANT TO REMEMBER ABOUT TODAY

I GIVE TODAY A

MY INTENTION FOR
TOMORROW

SOMETHING I COULD HAVE BEEN MORE GRATEFUL FOR TODAY

DAY 94

DAY   MONTH   YEAR

THREE THINGS I'M GRATEFUL FOR

I GIVE TODAY A

SOMETHING I WANT TO REMEMBER ABOUT TODAY

SOMETHING I COULD HAVE BEEN MORE GRATEFUL FOR TODAY

MY INTENTION FOR TOMORROW

DAY   MONTH   YEAR

THREE THINGS I'M GRATEFUL FOR

SOMETHING I WANT TO REMEMBER ABOUT TODAY   I GIVE TODAY A

MY INTENTION FOR   SOMETHING I COULD HAVE BEEN MORE GRATEFUL FOR TODAY
TOMORROW

DAY 96

DAY   MONTH   YEAR

THREE THINGS I'M GRATEFUL FOR

I GIVE TODAY A

SOMETHING I WANT TO REMEMBER ABOUT TODAY

SOMETHING I COULD HAVE BEEN MORE GRATEFUL FOR TODAY

MY INTENTION FOR
TOMORROW

DAY 97

THREE THINGS I'M GRATEFUL FOR

SOMETHING I WANT TO REMEMBER ABOUT TODAY

I GIVE TODAY A

MY INTENTION FOR
TOMORROW

SOMETHING I COULD HAVE BEEN MORE GRATEFUL FOR TODAY

DAY 98

DAY   MONTH   YEAR

THREE THINGS I'M GRATEFUL FOR

I GIVE TODAY A

SOMETHING I WANT TO REMEMBER ABOUT TODAY

SOMETHING I COULD HAVE BEEN MORE GRATEFUL FOR TODAY

MY INTENTION FOR TOMORROW

DAY 98

YOUR ABILITY TO SEE BEAUTY AND POSSIBILITY IS PROPORTIONATE
TO THE LEVEL AT WHICH YOU EMBRACE GRATITUDE.
STEVE MARABOLI

SOMETHING I COULD HAVE BEEN MORE GRATEFUL FOR THIS WEEK

I GIVE THIS WEEK A

SOMETHING I WANT TO REMEMBER ABOUT THIS WEEK

MY INTENTION FOR NEXT
WEEK

SOMEONE I COULD HAVE FELT MORE GRATEFUL FOR THIS WEEK

DAY   MONTH   YEAR

THREE THINGS I'M GRATEFUL FOR

I GIVE TODAY A

SOMETHING I WANT TO REMEMBER ABOUT TODAY

SOMETHING I COULD HAVE BEEN MORE GRATEFUL FOR TODAY

MY INTENTION FOR
TOMORROW

DAY   MONTH   YEAR

THREE THINGS I'M GRATEFUL FOR

SOMETHING I WANT TO REMEMBER ABOUT TODAY   I GIVE TODAY A

MY INTENTION FOR TOMORROW   SOMETHING I COULD HAVE BEEN MORE GRATEFUL FOR TODAY

DAY   MONTH   YEAR

THREE THINGS I'M GRATEFUL FOR

I GIVE TODAY A

SOMETHING I WANT TO REMEMBER ABOUT TODAY

SOMETHING I COULD HAVE BEEN MORE GRATEFUL FOR TODAY

MY INTENTION FOR
TOMORROW

DAY   MONTH   YEAR

THREE THINGS I'M GRATEFUL FOR

SOMETHING I WANT TO REMEMBER ABOUT TODAY   I GIVE TODAY A

MY INTENTION FOR   SOMETHING I COULD HAVE BEEN MORE GRATEFUL FOR TODAY
TOMORROW

DAY   MONTH   YEAR

THREE THINGS I'M GRATEFUL FOR

I GIVE TODAY A

SOMETHING I WANT TO REMEMBER ABOUT TODAY

SOMETHING I COULD HAVE BEEN MORE GRATEFUL FOR TODAY

MY INTENTION FOR TOMORROW

DAY 104

Day   Month   Year

Three things I'm grateful for

Something I want to remember about today

I give today a

My intention for
tomorrow

Something I could have been more grateful for today

DAY   MONTH   YEAR

THREE THINGS I'M GRATEFUL FOR

I GIVE TODAY A

SOMETHING I WANT TO REMEMBER ABOUT TODAY

SOMETHING I COULD HAVE BEEN MORE GRATEFUL FOR TODAY

MY INTENTION FOR TOMORROW

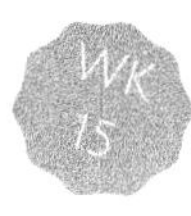

Gratitude is one of the strongest and most transformative states of being. It shifts your perspective from lack to abundance and allows you to focus on the good in your life, which in turn pulls more goodness into your reality.

Jen Sincero

SOMETHING I COULD HAVE BEEN MORE GRATEFUL FOR THIS WEEK

I GIVE THIS WEEK A

SOMETHING I WANT TO REMEMBER ABOUT THIS WEEK

MY INTENTION FOR NEXT WEEK

SOMEONE I COULD HAVE FELT MORE GRATEFUL FOR THIS WEEK

DAY 106

DAY   MONTH   YEAR

THREE THINGS I'M GRATEFUL FOR

I GIVE TODAY A

SOMETHING I WANT TO REMEMBER ABOUT TODAY

SOMETHING I COULD HAVE BEEN MORE GRATEFUL FOR TODAY

MY INTENTION FOR TOMORROW

DAY 107

Day   Month   Year

Three things I'm grateful for

Something I want to remember about today   I give today a

My intention for   Something I could have been more grateful for today
tomorrow

DAY 108

DAY   MONTH   YEAR

THREE THINGS I'M GRATEFUL FOR

I GIVE TODAY A

SOMETHING I WANT TO REMEMBER ABOUT TODAY

SOMETHING I COULD HAVE BEEN MORE GRATEFUL FOR TODAY

MY INTENTION FOR TOMORROW

DAY 109

THREE THINGS I'M GRATEFUL FOR

SOMETHING I WANT TO REMEMBER ABOUT TODAY

I GIVE TODAY A

MY INTENTION FOR
TOMORROW

SOMETHING I COULD HAVE BEEN MORE GRATEFUL FOR TODAY

DAY 110

DAY   MONTH   YEAR

THREE THINGS I'M GRATEFUL FOR

I GIVE TODAY A

SOMETHING I WANT TO REMEMBER ABOUT TODAY

SOMETHING I COULD HAVE BEEN MORE GRATEFUL FOR TODAY

MY INTENTION FOR
TOMORROW

DAY 111

DAY · MONTH · YEAR

THREE THINGS I'M GRATEFUL FOR

SOMETHING I WANT TO REMEMBER ABOUT TODAY

I GIVE TODAY A

MY INTENTION FOR TOMORROW

SOMETHING I COULD HAVE BEEN MORE GRATEFUL FOR TODAY

 # DAY 112 

DAY   MONTH   YEAR

THREE THINGS I'M GRATEFUL FOR

I GIVE TODAY A

SOMETHING I WANT TO REMEMBER ABOUT TODAY

SOMETHING I COULD HAVE BEEN MORE GRATEFUL FOR TODAY

MY INTENTION FOR
TOMORROW

DAY 112

THE SINGLE GREATEST THING YOU CAN DO TO CHANGE YOUR LIFE TODAY WOULD BE TO START BEING GRATEFUL FOR WHAT YOU HAVE RIGHT NOW.

Oprah Winfrey

SOMETHING I COULD HAVE BEEN MORE GRATEFUL FOR THESE PAST FOUR WEEKS

I GIVE THE PAST FOUR WEEKS A

SOMETHING I WANT TO REMEMBER ABOUT THE PAST FOUR WEEKS

MY INTENTION FOR THE NEXT FOUR WEEKS

SOMEONE I COULD HAVE FELT MORE GRATEFUL FOR THESE PAST FOUR WEEKS

DAY 113

DAY   MONTH   YEAR

THREE THINGS I'M GRATEFUL FOR

I GIVE TODAY A

SOMETHING I WANT TO REMEMBER ABOUT TODAY

SOMETHING I COULD HAVE BEEN MORE GRATEFUL FOR TODAY

MY INTENTION FOR TOMORROW

DAY 114

Day   Month   Year

Three things I'm grateful for

Something I want to remember about today   I give today a

My intention for tomorrow   Something I could have been more grateful for today

DAY 115

DAY   MONTH   YEAR

THREE THINGS I'M GRATEFUL FOR

I GIVE TODAY A

SOMETHING I WANT TO REMEMBER ABOUT TODAY

SOMETHING I COULD HAVE BEEN MORE GRATEFUL FOR TODAY

MY INTENTION FOR TOMORROW

DAY 116

DAY   MONTH   YEAR

THREE THINGS I'M GRATEFUL FOR

SOMETHING I WANT TO REMEMBER ABOUT TODAY

I GIVE TODAY A

MY INTENTION FOR
TOMORROW

SOMETHING I COULD HAVE BEEN MORE GRATEFUL FOR TODAY

DAY 117

DAY   MONTH   YEAR

THREE THINGS I'M GRATEFUL FOR

I GIVE TODAY A

SOMETHING I WANT TO REMEMBER ABOUT TODAY

SOMETHING I COULD HAVE BEEN MORE GRATEFUL FOR TODAY

MY INTENTION FOR
TOMORROW

DAY 118

Three things I'm grateful for

Something I want to remember about today

I give today a

My intention for tomorrow

Something I could have been more grateful for today

DAY 119

Day   Month   Year

Three things I'm grateful for

I GIVE TODAY A

Something I want to remember about today

Something I could have been more grateful for today

My intention for
tomorrow

DAY 119

WK 17

GRATITUDE HELPS US TO SEE WHAT IS THERE INSTEAD OF WHAT ISN'T.
Annette Bridges

SOMETHING I COULD HAVE BEEN MORE GRATEFUL FOR THIS WEEK

I GIVE THIS WEEK A

SOMETHING I WANT TO REMEMBER ABOUT THIS WEEK

MY INTENTION FOR NEXT WEEK

SOMEONE I COULD HAVE FELT MORE GRATEFUL FOR THIS WEEK

DAY 120

DAY   MONTH   YEAR

THREE THINGS I'M GRATEFUL FOR

I GIVE TODAY A

SOMETHING I WANT TO REMEMBER ABOUT TODAY

SOMETHING I COULD HAVE BEEN MORE GRATEFUL FOR TODAY

MY INTENTION FOR
TOMORROW

DAY 121

Day　　　　　Month　　　　　Year

Three things I'm grateful for

Something I want to remember about today　　　　　I give today a

My intention for
tomorrow　　　　　Something I could have been more grateful for today

DAY 122

DAY   MONTH   YEAR

THREE THINGS I'M GRATEFUL FOR

I GIVE TODAY A

SOMETHING I WANT TO REMEMBER ABOUT TODAY

SOMETHING I COULD HAVE BEEN MORE GRATEFUL FOR TODAY

MY INTENTION FOR TOMORROW

DAY 123

DAY   MONTH   YEAR

THREE THINGS I'M GRATEFUL FOR

SOMETHING I WANT TO REMEMBER ABOUT TODAY   I GIVE TODAY A

MY INTENTION FOR
TOMORROW   SOMETHING I COULD HAVE BEEN MORE GRATEFUL FOR TODAY

DAY 124

DAY   MONTH   YEAR

THREE THINGS I'M GRATEFUL FOR

I GIVE TODAY A

SOMETHING I WANT TO REMEMBER ABOUT TODAY

SOMETHING I COULD HAVE BEEN MORE GRATEFUL FOR TODAY

MY INTENTION FOR
TOMORROW

DAY 125

THREE THINGS I'M GRATEFUL FOR

SOMETHING I WANT TO REMEMBER ABOUT TODAY

I GIVE TODAY A

MY INTENTION FOR
TOMORROW

SOMETHING I COULD HAVE BEEN MORE GRATEFUL FOR TODAY

DAY 126

DAY   MONTH   YEAR

THREE THINGS I'M GRATEFUL FOR

I GIVE TODAY A

SOMETHING I WANT TO REMEMBER ABOUT TODAY

SOMETHING I COULD HAVE BEEN MORE GRATEFUL FOR TODAY

MY INTENTION FOR TOMORROW

IF YOU WANT TO KNOW HOW RICH YOU ARE, FIND OUT HOW MANY THINGS YOU HAVE THAT MONEY CANNOT BUY.

UNKNOWN

SOMETHING I COULD HAVE BEEN MORE GRATEFUL FOR THIS WEEK

I GIVE THIS WEEK A

SOMETHING I WANT TO REMEMBER ABOUT THIS WEEK

MY INTENTION FOR NEXT WEEK

SOMEONE I COULD HAVE FELT MORE GRATEFUL FOR THIS WEEK

DAY   MONTH   YEAR

THREE THINGS I'M GRATEFUL FOR

I GIVE TODAY A

SOMETHING I WANT TO REMEMBER ABOUT TODAY

SOMETHING I COULD HAVE BEEN MORE GRATEFUL FOR TODAY

MY INTENTION FOR TOMORROW

DAY 128

THREE THINGS I'M GRATEFUL FOR

SOMETHING I WANT TO REMEMBER ABOUT TODAY

I GIVE TODAY A

MY INTENTION FOR TOMORROW

SOMETHING I COULD HAVE BEEN MORE GRATEFUL FOR TODAY

DAY   MONTH   YEAR

THREE THINGS I'M GRATEFUL FOR

I GIVE TODAY A

SOMETHING I WANT TO REMEMBER ABOUT TODAY

SOMETHING I COULD HAVE BEEN MORE GRATEFUL FOR TODAY

MY INTENTION FOR TOMORROW

DAY   MONTH   YEAR

THREE THINGS I'M GRATEFUL FOR

SOMETHING I WANT TO REMEMBER ABOUT TODAY   I GIVE TODAY A

MY INTENTION FOR   SOMETHING I COULD HAVE BEEN MORE GRATEFUL FOR TODAY
TOMORROW

DAY   MONTH   YEAR

THREE THINGS I'M GRATEFUL FOR

I GIVE TODAY A

SOMETHING I WANT TO REMEMBER ABOUT TODAY

SOMETHING I COULD HAVE BEEN MORE GRATEFUL FOR TODAY

MY INTENTION FOR
TOMORROW

DAY   MONTH   YEAR

THREE THINGS I'M GRATEFUL FOR

SOMETHING I WANT TO REMEMBER ABOUT TODAY   I GIVE TODAY A

MY INTENTION FOR   SOMETHING I COULD HAVE BEEN MORE GRATEFUL FOR TODAY
TOMORROW

DAY	MONTH	YEAR

THREE THINGS I'M GRATEFUL FOR

I GIVE TODAY A

SOMETHING I WANT TO REMEMBER ABOUT TODAY

SOMETHING I COULD HAVE BEEN MORE GRATEFUL FOR TODAY

MY INTENTION FOR TOMORROW

WK 19

I DON'T HAVE TO CHASE EXTRAORDINARY MOMENTS TO FIND HAPPINESS—IT'S RIGHT IN FRONT OF ME IF I'M PAYING ATTENTION AND PRACTICING GRATITUDE.
BRENÉ BROWN

SOMETHING I COULD HAVE BEEN MORE GRATEFUL FOR THIS WEEK

I GIVE THIS WEEK A

SOMETHING I WANT TO REMEMBER ABOUT THIS WEEK

MY INTENTION FOR NEXT WEEK

SOMEONE I COULD HAVE FELT MORE GRATEFUL FOR THIS WEEK

DAY 134

DAY   MONTH   YEAR

THREE THINGS I'M GRATEFUL FOR

I GIVE TODAY A

SOMETHING I WANT TO REMEMBER ABOUT TODAY

SOMETHING I COULD HAVE BEEN MORE GRATEFUL FOR TODAY

MY INTENTION FOR
TOMORROW

DAY 135

DAY   MONTH   YEAR

THREE THINGS I'M GRATEFUL FOR

SOMETHING I WANT TO REMEMBER ABOUT TODAY

I GIVE TODAY A

MY INTENTION FOR TOMORROW

SOMETHING I COULD HAVE BEEN MORE GRATEFUL FOR TODAY

DAY 136

DAY   MONTH   YEAR

THREE THINGS I'M GRATEFUL FOR

I GIVE TODAY A

SOMETHING I WANT TO REMEMBER ABOUT TODAY

SOMETHING I COULD HAVE BEEN MORE GRATEFUL FOR TODAY

MY INTENTION FOR TOMORROW

Day   Month   Year

Three things I'm grateful for

Something I want to remember about today

I give today a

My intention for
tomorrow

Something I could have been more grateful for today

DAY 138

DAY   MONTH   YEAR

THREE THINGS I'M GRATEFUL FOR

I GIVE TODAY A

SOMETHING I WANT TO REMEMBER ABOUT TODAY

SOMETHING I COULD HAVE BEEN MORE GRATEFUL FOR TODAY

MY INTENTION FOR TOMORROW

DAY 139

Day   Month   Year

THREE THINGS I'M GRATEFUL FOR

Something I want to remember about today

I give today a

My intention for tomorrow

Something I could have been more grateful for today

DAY   MONTH   YEAR

THREE THINGS I'M GRATEFUL FOR

I GIVE TODAY A

SOMETHING I WANT TO REMEMBER ABOUT TODAY

SOMETHING I COULD HAVE BEEN MORE GRATEFUL FOR TODAY

MY INTENTION FOR TOMORROW

 # DAY 140 

LEARN TO BE THANKFUL FOR WHAT YOU ALREADY HAVE
WHILE YOU PURSUE ALL THAT YOU WANT.

Jim Rohn

SOMETHING I COULD HAVE BEEN MORE GRATEFUL FOR THESE
PAST FOUR WEEKS

I GIVE THE PAST FOUR WEEKS A

SOMETHING I WANT TO REMEMBER ABOUT THE PAST FOUR WEEKS

MY INTENTION FOR THE
NEXT FOUR WEEKS

SOMEONE I COULD HAVE FELT MORE GRATEFUL FOR THESE PAST
FOUR WEEKS

DAY 141

DAY MONTH YEAR

THREE THINGS I'M GRATEFUL FOR

I GIVE TODAY A

SOMETHING I WANT TO REMEMBER ABOUT TODAY

SOMETHING I COULD HAVE BEEN MORE GRATEFUL FOR TODAY

MY INTENTION FOR
TOMORROW

DAY 142

DAY   MONTH   YEAR

THREE THINGS I'M GRATEFUL FOR

SOMETHING I WANT TO REMEMBER ABOUT TODAY   I GIVE TODAY A

MY INTENTION FOR   SOMETHING I COULD HAVE BEEN MORE GRATEFUL FOR TODAY
TOMORROW

DAY 143

DAY   MONTH   YEAR

THREE THINGS I'M GRATEFUL FOR

I GIVE TODAY A

SOMETHING I WANT TO REMEMBER ABOUT TODAY

SOMETHING I COULD HAVE BEEN MORE GRATEFUL FOR TODAY

MY INTENTION FOR TOMORROW

DAY 144

DAY   MONTH   YEAR

THREE THINGS I'M GRATEFUL FOR

SOMETHING I WANT TO REMEMBER ABOUT TODAY   I GIVE TODAY A

MY INTENTION FOR
TOMORROW   SOMETHING I COULD HAVE BEEN MORE GRATEFUL FOR TODAY

DAY 145

DAY   MONTH   YEAR

THREE THINGS I'M GRATEFUL FOR

I GIVE TODAY A

SOMETHING I WANT TO REMEMBER ABOUT TODAY

SOMETHING I COULD HAVE BEEN MORE GRATEFUL FOR TODAY

MY INTENTION FOR
TOMORROW

DAY 146

THREE THINGS I'M GRATEFUL FOR

SOMETHING I WANT TO REMEMBER ABOUT TODAY

I GIVE TODAY A

MY INTENTION FOR TOMORROW

SOMETHING I COULD HAVE BEEN MORE GRATEFUL FOR TODAY

DAY 147

DAY   MONTH   YEAR

THREE THINGS I'M GRATEFUL FOR

I GIVE TODAY A

SOMETHING I WANT TO REMEMBER ABOUT TODAY

SOMETHING I COULD HAVE BEEN MORE GRATEFUL FOR TODAY

MY INTENTION FOR TOMORROW

WK 21

IF YOU MUST LOOK BACK, DO SO FORGIVINGLY. IF YOU MUST LOOK FORWARD, DO SO PRAYERFULLY. HOWEVER, THE WISEST THING YOU CAN DO IS BE PRESENT IN THE PRESENT... GRATEFULLY.

MAYA ANGELOU

SOMETHING I COULD HAVE BEEN MORE GRATEFUL FOR THIS WEEK

I GIVE THIS WEEK A

SOMETHING I WANT TO REMEMBER ABOUT THIS WEEK

MY INTENTION FOR NEXT WEEK

SOMEONE I COULD HAVE FELT MORE GRATEFUL FOR THIS WEEK

DAY 148

DAY   MONTH   YEAR

THREE THINGS I'M GRATEFUL FOR

I GIVE TODAY A

SOMETHING I WANT TO REMEMBER ABOUT TODAY

SOMETHING I COULD HAVE BEEN MORE GRATEFUL FOR TODAY

MY INTENTION FOR TOMORROW

DAY 149

DAY   MONTH   YEAR

Three things I'm grateful for

Something I want to remember about today

I give today a

My intention for
tomorrow

Something I could have been more grateful for today

DAY 150

DAY   MONTH   YEAR

THREE THINGS I'M GRATEFUL FOR

I GIVE TODAY A

SOMETHING I WANT TO REMEMBER ABOUT TODAY

SOMETHING I COULD HAVE BEEN MORE GRATEFUL FOR TODAY

MY INTENTION FOR TOMORROW

DAY   MONTH   YEAR

THREE THINGS I'M GRATEFUL FOR

SOMETHING I WANT TO REMEMBER ABOUT TODAY

I GIVE TODAY A

MY INTENTION FOR
TOMORROW

SOMETHING I COULD HAVE BEEN MORE GRATEFUL FOR TODAY

DAY 152

DAY   MONTH   YEAR

THREE THINGS I'M GRATEFUL FOR

I GIVE TODAY A

SOMETHING I WANT TO REMEMBER ABOUT TODAY

SOMETHING I COULD HAVE BEEN MORE GRATEFUL FOR TODAY

MY INTENTION FOR
TOMORROW

DAY 153

DAY   MONTH   YEAR

THREE THINGS I'M GRATEFUL FOR

SOMETHING I WANT TO REMEMBER ABOUT TODAY   I GIVE TODAY A

MY INTENTION FOR
TOMORROW   SOMETHING I COULD HAVE BEEN MORE GRATEFUL FOR TODAY

DAY 154

DAY   MONTH   YEAR

THREE THINGS I'M GRATEFUL FOR

I GIVE TODAY A

SOMETHING I WANT TO REMEMBER ABOUT TODAY

SOMETHING I COULD HAVE BEEN MORE GRATEFUL FOR TODAY

MY INTENTION FOR
TOMORROW

WK 22

Happiness isn't about getting what you want all the time. It's about loving what you have and being grateful for it.

UNKNOWN

Something I could have been more grateful for this week

I give this week a

Something I want to remember about this week

My intention for next week

Someone I could have felt more grateful for this week

DAY   MONTH   YEAR

THREE THINGS I'M GRATEFUL FOR

I GIVE TODAY A

SOMETHING I WANT TO REMEMBER ABOUT TODAY

SOMETHING I COULD HAVE BEEN MORE GRATEFUL FOR TODAY

MY INTENTION FOR
TOMORROW

DAY 156

DAY   MONTH   YEAR

THREE THINGS I'M GRATEFUL FOR

SOMETHING I WANT TO REMEMBER ABOUT TODAY

I GIVE TODAY A

MY INTENTION FOR TOMORROW

SOMETHING I COULD HAVE BEEN MORE GRATEFUL FOR TODAY

DAY   MONTH   YEAR

THREE THINGS I'M GRATEFUL FOR

I GIVE TODAY A

SOMETHING I WANT TO REMEMBER ABOUT TODAY

SOMETHING I COULD HAVE BEEN MORE GRATEFUL FOR TODAY

MY INTENTION FOR TOMORROW

DAY   MONTH   YEAR

THREE THINGS I'M GRATEFUL FOR

SOMETHING I WANT TO REMEMBER ABOUT TODAY   I GIVE TODAY A

MY INTENTION FOR   SOMETHING I COULD HAVE BEEN MORE GRATEFUL FOR TODAY
TOMORROW

DAY   MONTH   YEAR

THREE THINGS I'M GRATEFUL FOR

I GIVE TODAY A

SOMETHING I WANT TO REMEMBER ABOUT TODAY

SOMETHING I COULD HAVE BEEN MORE GRATEFUL FOR TODAY

MY INTENTION FOR
TOMORROW

DAY   MONTH   YEAR

THREE THINGS I'M GRATEFUL FOR

SOMETHING I WANT TO REMEMBER ABOUT TODAY   I GIVE TODAY A

MY INTENTION FOR   SOMETHING I COULD HAVE BEEN MORE GRATEFUL FOR TODAY
TOMORROW

DAY	MONTH	YEAR

THREE THINGS I'M GRATEFUL FOR

I GIVE TODAY A

SOMETHING I WANT TO REMEMBER ABOUT TODAY

SOMETHING I COULD HAVE BEEN MORE GRATEFUL FOR TODAY

MY INTENTION FOR TOMORROW

DAY 161

HAPPINESS WILL NEVER COME TO THOSE WHO FAIL TO APPRECIATE WHAT THEY ALREADY HAVE.

BUDDHA

SOMETHING I COULD HAVE BEEN MORE GRATEFUL FOR THIS WEEK

I GIVE THIS WEEK A

SOMETHING I WANT TO REMEMBER ABOUT THIS WEEK

MY INTENTION FOR NEXT WEEK

SOMEONE I COULD HAVE FELT MORE GRATEFUL FOR THIS WEEK

DAY 162

THREE THINGS I'M GRATEFUL FOR

I GIVE TODAY A

SOMETHING I WANT TO REMEMBER ABOUT TODAY

SOMETHING I COULD HAVE BEEN MORE GRATEFUL FOR TODAY

MY INTENTION FOR
TOMORROW

 # DAY 163 

Day　　　　Month　　　　Year

Three things I'm grateful for

Something I want to remember about today

I give today a

My intention for
tomorrow

Something I could have been more grateful for today

 # DAY 164 

DAY   MONTH   YEAR

THREE THINGS I'M GRATEFUL FOR

I GIVE TODAY A

SOMETHING I WANT TO REMEMBER ABOUT TODAY

SOMETHING I COULD HAVE BEEN MORE GRATEFUL FOR TODAY

MY INTENTION FOR TOMORROW

DAY 165

DAY MONTH YEAR

THREE THINGS I'M GRATEFUL FOR

SOMETHING I WANT TO REMEMBER ABOUT TODAY I GIVE TODAY A

MY INTENTION FOR
TOMORROW SOMETHING I COULD HAVE BEEN MORE GRATEFUL FOR TODAY

DAY 166

DAY MONTH YEAR

THREE THINGS I'M GRATEFUL FOR

I GIVE TODAY A

SOMETHING I WANT TO REMEMBER ABOUT TODAY

SOMETHING I COULD HAVE BEEN MORE GRATEFUL FOR TODAY

MY INTENTION FOR TOMORROW

DAY 167

DAY   MONTH   YEAR

THREE THINGS I'M GRATEFUL FOR

SOMETHING I WANT TO REMEMBER ABOUT TODAY   I GIVE TODAY A

MY INTENTION FOR   SOMETHING I COULD HAVE BEEN MORE GRATEFUL FOR TODAY
TOMORROW

DAY 168

DAY   MONTH   YEAR

THREE THINGS I'M GRATEFUL FOR

I GIVE TODAY A

SOMETHING I WANT TO REMEMBER ABOUT TODAY

SOMETHING I COULD HAVE BEEN MORE GRATEFUL FOR TODAY

MY INTENTION FOR TOMORROW

 # DAY 168 

Walking the grounds of gratitude
I stumbled upon the palace of happiness.

Brendon Burchard

SOMETHING I COULD HAVE BEEN MORE GRATEFUL FOR THESE PAST FOUR WEEKS

I GIVE THE PAST FOUR WEEKS A

SOMETHING I WANT TO REMEMBER ABOUT THE PAST FOUR WEEKS

MY INTENTION FOR THE NEXT FOUR WEEKS

SOMEONE I COULD HAVE FELT MORE GRATEFUL FOR THESE PAST FOUR WEEKS

DAY 169

DAY   MONTH   YEAR

THREE THINGS I'M GRATEFUL FOR

I GIVE TODAY A

SOMETHING I WANT TO REMEMBER ABOUT TODAY

SOMETHING I COULD HAVE BEEN MORE GRATEFUL FOR TODAY

MY INTENTION FOR
TOMORROW

DAY 170

DAY MONTH YEAR

THREE THINGS I'M GRATEFUL FOR

SOMETHING I WANT TO REMEMBER ABOUT TODAY

I GIVE TODAY A

MY INTENTION FOR TOMORROW

SOMETHING I COULD HAVE BEEN MORE GRATEFUL FOR TODAY

DAY 171

DAY   MONTH   YEAR

THREE THINGS I'M GRATEFUL FOR

I GIVE TODAY A

SOMETHING I WANT TO REMEMBER ABOUT TODAY

SOMETHING I COULD HAVE BEEN MORE GRATEFUL FOR TODAY

MY INTENTION FOR TOMORROW

DAY 172

Day   Month   Year

Three things I'm grateful for

Something I want to remember about today

I give today a

My intention for tomorrow

Something I could have been more grateful for today

DAY 173

DAY   MONTH   YEAR

THREE THINGS I'M GRATEFUL FOR

I GIVE TODAY A

SOMETHING I WANT TO REMEMBER ABOUT TODAY

SOMETHING I COULD HAVE BEEN MORE GRATEFUL FOR TODAY

MY INTENTION FOR
TOMORROW

# DAY 174

Three things I'm grateful for

Something I want to remember about today

I give today a

My intention for tomorrow

Something I could have been more grateful for today

DAY 175

THREE THINGS I'M GRATEFUL FOR

I GIVE TODAY A

SOMETHING I WANT TO REMEMBER ABOUT TODAY

SOMETHING I COULD HAVE BEEN MORE GRATEFUL FOR TODAY

MY INTENTION FOR
TOMORROW

GRATITUDE IS THE RICH SOIL YOU PLANT YOUR FUTURE IN.

LISA NICHOLS

WK 25

SOMETHING I COULD HAVE BEEN MORE GRATEFUL FOR THIS WEEK

I GIVE THIS WEEK A

SOMETHING I WANT TO REMEMBER ABOUT THIS WEEK

MY INTENTION FOR NEXT WEEK

SOMEONE I COULD HAVE FELT MORE GRATEFUL FOR THIS WEEK

DAY 176

DAY   MONTH   YEAR

THREE THINGS I'M GRATEFUL FOR

I GIVE TODAY A

SOMETHING I WANT TO REMEMBER ABOUT TODAY

SOMETHING I COULD HAVE BEEN MORE GRATEFUL FOR TODAY

MY INTENTION FOR TOMORROW

DAY 177

THREE THINGS I'M GRATEFUL FOR

SOMETHING I WANT TO REMEMBER ABOUT TODAY

I GIVE TODAY A

MY INTENTION FOR TOMORROW

SOMETHING I COULD HAVE BEEN MORE GRATEFUL FOR TODAY

DAY 178

THREE THINGS I'M GRATEFUL FOR

I GIVE TODAY A

SOMETHING I WANT TO REMEMBER ABOUT TODAY

SOMETHING I COULD HAVE BEEN MORE GRATEFUL FOR TODAY

MY INTENTION FOR
TOMORROW

DAY 179

DAY   MONTH   YEAR

THREE THINGS I'M GRATEFUL FOR

SOMETHING I WANT TO REMEMBER ABOUT TODAY   I GIVE TODAY A

MY INTENTION FOR
TOMORROW   SOMETHING I COULD HAVE BEEN MORE GRATEFUL FOR TODAY

DAY 180

DAY   MONTH   YEAR

THREE THINGS I'M GRATEFUL FOR

I GIVE TODAY A

SOMETHING I WANT TO REMEMBER ABOUT TODAY

SOMETHING I COULD HAVE BEEN MORE GRATEFUL FOR TODAY

MY INTENTION FOR
TOMORROW

DAY 181

THREE THINGS I'M GRATEFUL FOR

SOMETHING I WANT TO REMEMBER ABOUT TODAY

I GIVE TODAY A

MY INTENTION FOR
TOMORROW

SOMETHING I COULD HAVE BEEN MORE GRATEFUL FOR TODAY

DAY 182

DAY   MONTH   YEAR

THREE THINGS I'M GRATEFUL FOR

I GIVE TODAY A

SOMETHING I WANT TO REMEMBER ABOUT TODAY

SOMETHING I COULD HAVE BEEN MORE GRATEFUL FOR TODAY

MY INTENTION FOR TOMORROW

DAY 182

TAKE A STEP BACK TODAY. LOOK AT ALL THOSE BEAUTIFUL THINGS YOU HAVE.

UNKNOWN

SOMETHING I COULD HAVE BEEN MORE GRATEFUL FOR THIS WEEK

I GIVE THIS WEEK A

SOMETHING I WANT TO REMEMBER ABOUT THIS WEEK

MY INTENTION FOR NEXT WEEK

SOMEONE I COULD HAVE FELT MORE GRATEFUL FOR THIS WEEK

Let's look back again. Go over the past thirteen weeks, then answer the following:

Something I want to remember about the past three months

Looking back over the past three months, I am most grateful for

The biggest lesson I learned over the past three months

Someone or something I could have felt more grateful for during the past three months

6 MONTHS

I GIVE THE PAST THREE MONTHS A

WHAT HAVE I BEEN UNABLE TO FEEL GRATEFUL FOR DURING THE PAST THREE MONTHS? CAN I REFORMULATE THAT THOUGHT ANYWAY?

I AM GRATEFUL......

WHEN LOOKING BACK ON HOW I'VE RATED MY WEEKS THUS FAR, THE NUMBERS TELL ME

MY INTENTION FOR THE NEXT THREE MONTHS

WHO HAVE I BEEN UNABLE TO FEEL GRATEFUL FOR DURING THE PAST THREE MONTHS? CAN I REFORMULATE THAT THOUGHT ANYWAY? I AM GRATEFUL......

DAY   MONTH   YEAR

THREE THINGS I'M GRATEFUL FOR

I GIVE TODAY A

SOMETHING I WANT TO REMEMBER ABOUT TODAY

SOMETHING I COULD HAVE BEEN MORE GRATEFUL FOR TODAY

MY INTENTION FOR TOMORROW

DAY   MONTH   YEAR

THREE THINGS I'M GRATEFUL FOR

SOMETHING I WANT TO REMEMBER ABOUT TODAY   I GIVE TODAY A

MY INTENTION FOR   SOMETHING I COULD HAVE BEEN MORE GRATEFUL FOR TODAY
TOMORROW

DAY   MONTH   YEAR

THREE THINGS I'M GRATEFUL FOR

I GIVE TODAY A

SOMETHING I WANT TO REMEMBER ABOUT TODAY

SOMETHING I COULD HAVE BEEN MORE GRATEFUL FOR TODAY

MY INTENTION FOR TOMORROW

DAY   MONTH   YEAR

THREE THINGS I'M GRATEFUL FOR

SOMETHING I WANT TO REMEMBER ABOUT TODAY   I GIVE TODAY A

MY INTENTION FOR
TOMORROW   SOMETHING I COULD HAVE BEEN MORE GRATEFUL FOR TODAY

DAY   MONTH   YEAR

THREE THINGS I'M GRATEFUL FOR

I GIVE TODAY A

SOMETHING I WANT TO REMEMBER ABOUT TODAY

SOMETHING I COULD HAVE BEEN MORE GRATEFUL FOR TODAY

MY INTENTION FOR TOMORROW

DAY   MONTH   YEAR

THREE THINGS I'M GRATEFUL FOR

SOMETHING I WANT TO REMEMBER ABOUT TODAY   I GIVE TODAY A

MY INTENTION FOR
TOMORROW   SOMETHING I COULD HAVE BEEN MORE GRATEFUL FOR TODAY

DAY   MONTH   YEAR

THREE THINGS I'M GRATEFUL FOR

I GIVE TODAY A

SOMETHING I WANT TO REMEMBER ABOUT TODAY

SOMETHING I COULD HAVE BEEN MORE GRATEFUL FOR TODAY

MY INTENTION FOR
TOMORROW

DAY 189

BE HAPPY IN THE MOMENT, THAT'S ENOUGH.
EACH MOMENT IS ALL WE NEED, NOT MORE.

MOTHER TERESA

SOMETHING I COULD HAVE BEEN MORE GRATEFUL FOR THIS WEEK

I GIVE THIS WEEK A

SOMETHING I WANT TO REMEMBER ABOUT THIS WEEK

MY INTENTION FOR NEXT
WEEK

SOMEONE I COULD HAVE FELT MORE GRATEFUL FOR THIS WEEK

DAY   MONTH   YEAR

THREE THINGS I'M GRATEFUL FOR

I GIVE TODAY A

SOMETHING I WANT TO REMEMBER ABOUT TODAY

SOMETHING I COULD HAVE BEEN MORE GRATEFUL FOR TODAY

MY INTENTION FOR TOMORROW

DAY 191

MONTH

YEAR

THREE THINGS I'M GRATEFUL FOR

SOMETHING I WANT TO REMEMBER ABOUT TODAY

I GIVE TODAY A

MY INTENTION FOR
TOMORROW

SOMETHING I COULD HAVE BEEN MORE GRATEFUL FOR TODAY

DAY 192

DAY   MONTH   YEAR

THREE THINGS I'M GRATEFUL FOR

I GIVE TODAY A

SOMETHING I WANT TO REMEMBER ABOUT TODAY

SOMETHING I COULD HAVE BEEN MORE GRATEFUL FOR TODAY

MY INTENTION FOR TOMORROW

DAY 193

DAY   MONTH   YEAR

THREE THINGS I'M GRATEFUL FOR

SOMETHING I WANT TO REMEMBER ABOUT TODAY

I GIVE TODAY A

MY INTENTION FOR
TOMORROW

SOMETHING I COULD HAVE BEEN MORE GRATEFUL FOR TODAY

DAY 194

| DAY | MONTH | YEAR |

THREE THINGS I'M GRATEFUL FOR

I GIVE TODAY A

SOMETHING I WANT TO REMEMBER ABOUT TODAY

SOMETHING I COULD HAVE BEEN MORE GRATEFUL FOR TODAY

MY INTENTION FOR TOMORROW

 # DAY 195 

THREE THINGS I'M GRATEFUL FOR

SOMETHING I WANT TO REMEMBER ABOUT TODAY

I GIVE TODAY A

MY INTENTION FOR
TOMORROW

SOMETHING I COULD HAVE BEEN MORE GRATEFUL FOR TODAY

DAY 196

DAY   MONTH   YEAR

THREE THINGS I'M GRATEFUL FOR

I GIVE TODAY A

SOMETHING I WANT TO REMEMBER ABOUT TODAY

SOMETHING I COULD HAVE BEEN MORE GRATEFUL FOR TODAY

MY INTENTION FOR
TOMORROW

DAY 196

WHEN I STARTED COUNTING MY BLESSINGS, MY WHOLE LIFE TURNED AROUND.

WILLIE NELSON

SOMETHING I COULD HAVE BEEN MORE GRATEFUL FOR THESE PAST FOUR WEEKS

I GIVE THE PAST FOUR WEEKS A

SOMETHING I WANT TO REMEMBER ABOUT THE PAST FOUR WEEKS

MY INTENTION FOR THE NEXT FOUR WEEKS

SOMEONE I COULD HAVE FELT MORE GRATEFUL FOR THESE PAST FOUR WEEKS

DAY 197

DAY   MONTH   YEAR

THREE THINGS I'M GRATEFUL FOR

I GIVE TODAY A

SOMETHING I WANT TO REMEMBER ABOUT TODAY

SOMETHING I COULD HAVE BEEN MORE GRATEFUL FOR TODAY

MY INTENTION FOR TOMORROW

DAY 198

DAY
MONTH
YEAR

THREE THINGS I'M GRATEFUL FOR

SOMETHING I WANT TO REMEMBER ABOUT TODAY

I GIVE TODAY A

MY INTENTION FOR
TOMORROW

SOMETHING I COULD HAVE BEEN MORE GRATEFUL FOR TODAY

DAY 199

DAY   MONTH   YEAR

THREE THINGS I'M GRATEFUL FOR

I GIVE TODAY A

SOMETHING I WANT TO REMEMBER ABOUT TODAY

SOMETHING I COULD HAVE BEEN MORE GRATEFUL FOR TODAY

MY INTENTION FOR TOMORROW

DAY 200

THREE THINGS I'M GRATEFUL FOR

SOMETHING I WANT TO REMEMBER ABOUT TODAY

I GIVE TODAY A

MY INTENTION FOR
TOMORROW

SOMETHING I COULD HAVE BEEN MORE GRATEFUL FOR TODAY

DAY   MONTH   YEAR

THREE THINGS I'M GRATEFUL FOR

I GIVE TODAY A

SOMETHING I WANT TO REMEMBER ABOUT TODAY

SOMETHING I COULD HAVE BEEN MORE GRATEFUL FOR TODAY

MY INTENTION FOR TOMORROW

DAY 202

THREE THINGS I'M GRATEFUL FOR

SOMETHING I WANT TO REMEMBER ABOUT TODAY

I GIVE TODAY A

MY INTENTION FOR
TOMORROW

SOMETHING I COULD HAVE BEEN MORE GRATEFUL FOR TODAY

DAY MONTH YEAR

THREE THINGS I'M GRATEFUL FOR

I GIVE TODAY A

SOMETHING I WANT TO REMEMBER ABOUT TODAY

SOMETHING I COULD HAVE BEEN MORE GRATEFUL FOR TODAY

MY INTENTION FOR TOMORROW

WHEN ASKED IF MY CUP IS HALF FULL OR HALF EMPTY,
MY ONLY RESPONSE IS THAT I AM THANKFUL I HAVE A CUP.
SAM LEFKOWITZ

SOMETHING I COULD HAVE BEEN MORE GRATEFUL FOR THIS WEEK

I GIVE THIS WEEK A

SOMETHING I WANT TO REMEMBER ABOUT THIS WEEK

MY INTENTION FOR NEXT WEEK

SOMEONE I COULD HAVE FELT MORE GRATEFUL FOR THIS WEEK

DAY 204

DAY   MONTH   YEAR

THREE THINGS I'M GRATEFUL FOR

I GIVE TODAY A

SOMETHING I WANT TO REMEMBER ABOUT TODAY

SOMETHING I COULD HAVE BEEN MORE GRATEFUL FOR TODAY

MY INTENTION FOR TOMORROW

DAY 205

DAY   MONTH   YEAR

THREE THINGS I'M GRATEFUL FOR

SOMETHING I WANT TO REMEMBER ABOUT TODAY

I GIVE TODAY A

MY INTENTION FOR TOMORROW

SOMETHING I COULD HAVE BEEN MORE GRATEFUL FOR TODAY

DAY 206

DAY   MONTH   YEAR

THREE THINGS I'M GRATEFUL FOR

I GIVE TODAY A

SOMETHING I WANT TO REMEMBER ABOUT TODAY

SOMETHING I COULD HAVE BEEN MORE GRATEFUL FOR TODAY

MY INTENTION FOR
TOMORROW

DAY 207

THREE THINGS I'M GRATEFUL FOR

SOMETHING I WANT TO REMEMBER ABOUT TODAY

I GIVE TODAY A

MY INTENTION FOR
TOMORROW

SOMETHING I COULD HAVE BEEN MORE GRATEFUL FOR TODAY

DAY 208

THREE THINGS I'M GRATEFUL FOR

I GIVE TODAY A

SOMETHING I WANT TO REMEMBER ABOUT TODAY

SOMETHING I COULD HAVE BEEN MORE GRATEFUL FOR TODAY

MY INTENTION FOR
TOMORROW

DAY MONTH YEAR

THREE THINGS I'M GRATEFUL FOR

SOMETHING I WANT TO REMEMBER ABOUT TODAY

I GIVE TODAY A

MY INTENTION FOR TOMORROW

SOMETHING I COULD HAVE BEEN MORE GRATEFUL FOR TODAY

DAY 210

THREE THINGS I'M GRATEFUL FOR

I GIVE TODAY A

SOMETHING I WANT TO REMEMBER ABOUT TODAY

SOMETHING I COULD HAVE BEEN MORE GRATEFUL FOR TODAY

MY INTENTION FOR
TOMORROW

The moment you start acting like life is a blessing
it starts feeling like one.

UNKNOWN

SOMETHING I COULD HAVE BEEN MORE GRATEFUL FOR THIS WEEK

I GIVE THIS WEEK A

SOMETHING I WANT TO REMEMBER ABOUT THIS WEEK

MY INTENTION FOR NEXT
WEEK

SOMEONE I COULD HAVE FELT MORE GRATEFUL FOR THIS WEEK

DAY   MONTH   YEAR

THREE THINGS I'M GRATEFUL FOR

I GIVE TODAY A

SOMETHING I WANT TO REMEMBER ABOUT TODAY

SOMETHING I COULD HAVE BEEN MORE GRATEFUL FOR TODAY

MY INTENTION FOR
TOMORROW

DAY   MONTH   YEAR

THREE THINGS I'M GRATEFUL FOR

SOMETHING I WANT TO REMEMBER ABOUT TODAY

I GIVE TODAY A

MY INTENTION FOR TOMORROW

SOMETHING I COULD HAVE BEEN MORE GRATEFUL FOR TODAY

DAY　　　MONTH　　　YEAR

THREE THINGS I'M GRATEFUL FOR

I GIVE TODAY A

SOMETHING I WANT TO REMEMBER ABOUT TODAY

SOMETHING I COULD HAVE BEEN MORE GRATEFUL FOR TODAY

MY INTENTION FOR TOMORROW

DAY   MONTH   YEAR

THREE THINGS I'M GRATEFUL FOR

I GIVE TODAY A

SOMETHING I WANT TO REMEMBER ABOUT TODAY

SOMETHING I COULD HAVE BEEN MORE GRATEFUL FOR TODAY

MY INTENTION FOR TOMORROW

DAY   MONTH   YEAR

THREE THINGS I'M GRATEFUL FOR

SOMETHING I WANT TO REMEMBER ABOUT TODAY   I GIVE TODAY A

MY INTENTION FOR   SOMETHING I COULD HAVE BEEN MORE GRATEFUL FOR TODAY
TOMORROW

DAY 217

DAY   MONTH   YEAR

THREE THINGS I'M GRATEFUL FOR

I GIVE TODAY A

SOMETHING I WANT TO REMEMBER ABOUT TODAY

SOMETHING I COULD HAVE BEEN MORE GRATEFUL FOR TODAY

MY INTENTION FOR TOMORROW

Happiness is letting go of what you think your life is supposed to look like and celebrating it for everything that it is.

Mandy Hale

Something I could have been more grateful for this week

I give this week a

Something I want to remember about this week

My intention for next week

Someone I could have felt more grateful for this week

DAY MONTH YEAR

THREE THINGS I'M GRATEFUL FOR

I GIVE TODAY A

SOMETHING I WANT TO REMEMBER ABOUT TODAY

SOMETHING I COULD HAVE BEEN MORE GRATEFUL FOR TODAY

MY INTENTION FOR TOMORROW

DAY 219

Day　　　　Month　　　　Year

Three things I'm grateful for

Something I want to remember about today

I give today a

My intention for
tomorrow

Something I could have been more grateful for today

DAY 220

DAY   MONTH   YEAR

THREE THINGS I'M GRATEFUL FOR

I GIVE TODAY A

SOMETHING I WANT TO REMEMBER ABOUT TODAY

SOMETHING I COULD HAVE BEEN MORE GRATEFUL FOR TODAY

MY INTENTION FOR
TOMORROW

DAY 221

THREE THINGS I'M GRATEFUL FOR

SOMETHING I WANT TO REMEMBER ABOUT TODAY

I GIVE TODAY A

MY INTENTION FOR
TOMORROW

SOMETHING I COULD HAVE BEEN MORE GRATEFUL FOR TODAY

DAY 222

DAY   MONTH   YEAR

THREE THINGS I'M GRATEFUL FOR

I GIVE TODAY A

SOMETHING I WANT TO REMEMBER ABOUT TODAY

SOMETHING I COULD HAVE BEEN MORE GRATEFUL FOR TODAY

MY INTENTION FOR TOMORROW

DAY 223

THREE THINGS I'M GRATEFUL FOR

SOMETHING I WANT TO REMEMBER ABOUT TODAY

I GIVE TODAY A

MY INTENTION FOR
TOMORROW

SOMETHING I COULD HAVE BEEN MORE GRATEFUL FOR TODAY

DAY 224

DAY   MONTH   YEAR

THREE THINGS I'M GRATEFUL FOR

I GIVE TODAY A

SOMETHING I WANT TO REMEMBER ABOUT TODAY

SOMETHING I COULD HAVE BEEN MORE GRATEFUL FOR TODAY

MY INTENTION FOR TOMORROW

DAY 224

I HAVE NOTICED THAT THE UNIVERSE LOVES GRATITUDE. THE MORE GRATEFUL YOU ARE, THE MORE GOODIES YOU GET. WHEN I SAY 'GOODIES' I DON'T MEAN ONLY MATERIAL THINGS. I MEAN ALL THE PEOPLE, PLACES, AND EXPERIENCES THAT MAKE LIFE SO WONDERFULLY WORTH LIVING.
LOUISE HAY

SOMETHING I COULD HAVE BEEN MORE GRATEFUL FOR THESE PAST FOUR WEEKS

I GIVE THE PAST FOUR WEEKS A

SOMETHING I WANT TO REMEMBER ABOUT THE PAST FOUR WEEKS

MY INTENTION FOR THE NEXT FOUR WEEKS

SOMEONE I COULD HAVE FELT MORE GRATEFUL FOR THESE PAST FOUR WEEKS

DAY 225

DAY   MONTH   YEAR

THREE THINGS I'M GRATEFUL FOR

I GIVE TODAY A

SOMETHING I WANT TO REMEMBER ABOUT TODAY

SOMETHING I COULD HAVE BEEN MORE GRATEFUL FOR TODAY

MY INTENTION FOR TOMORROW

Day 226

Day   Month   Year

Three things I'm grateful for

Something I want to remember about today

I give today a

My intention for tomorrow

Something I could have been more grateful for today

Day 227

Day   Month   Year

Three things I'm grateful for

I give today a

Something I want to remember about today

Something I could have been more grateful for today

My intention for tomorrow

Day 228

Three things I'm grateful for

Something I want to remember about today

I give today a

My intention for
tomorrow

Something I could have been more grateful for today

DAY 229

DAY   MONTH   YEAR

THREE THINGS I'M GRATEFUL FOR

I GIVE TODAY A

SOMETHING I WANT TO REMEMBER ABOUT TODAY

SOMETHING I COULD HAVE BEEN MORE GRATEFUL FOR TODAY

MY INTENTION FOR TOMORROW

DAY 230

THREE THINGS I'M GRATEFUL FOR

SOMETHING I WANT TO REMEMBER ABOUT TODAY

I GIVE TODAY A

MY INTENTION FOR
TOMORROW

SOMETHING I COULD HAVE BEEN MORE GRATEFUL FOR TODAY

DAY 231

DAY   MONTH   YEAR

THREE THINGS I'M GRATEFUL FOR

I GIVE TODAY A

SOMETHING I WANT TO REMEMBER ABOUT TODAY

SOMETHING I COULD HAVE BEEN MORE GRATEFUL FOR TODAY

MY INTENTION FOR
TOMORROW

DAY 231

IF YOU AREN'T GRATEFUL FOR WHAT YOU ALREADY HAVE,
WHAT MAKES YOU THINK YOU WOULD BE HAPPY WITH MORE?

POY T. BENNETT

SOMETHING I COULD HAVE BEEN MORE GRATEFUL FOR THIS WEEK

I GIVE THIS WEEK A

SOMETHING I WANT TO REMEMBER ABOUT THIS WEEK

MY INTENTION FOR NEXT
WEEK

SOMEONE I COULD HAVE FELT MORE GRATEFUL FOR THIS WEEK

DAY 232

DAY   MONTH   YEAR

THREE THINGS I'M GRATEFUL FOR

I GIVE TODAY A

SOMETHING I WANT TO REMEMBER ABOUT TODAY

SOMETHING I COULD HAVE BEEN MORE GRATEFUL FOR TODAY

MY INTENTION FOR TOMORROW

DAY 233

Day   Month   Year

Three things I'm grateful for

Something I want to remember about today

I give today a

My intention for
tomorrow

Something I could have been more grateful for today

DAY 234

DAY   MONTH   YEAR

THREE THINGS I'M GRATEFUL FOR

I GIVE TODAY A

SOMETHING I WANT TO REMEMBER ABOUT TODAY

SOMETHING I COULD HAVE BEEN MORE GRATEFUL FOR TODAY

MY INTENTION FOR TOMORROW

DAY   MONTH   YEAR

THREE THINGS I'M GRATEFUL FOR

SOMETHING I WANT TO REMEMBER ABOUT TODAY

I GIVE TODAY A

MY INTENTION FOR
TOMORROW

SOMETHING I COULD HAVE BEEN MORE GRATEFUL FOR TODAY

DAY 236

DAY   MONTH   YEAR

THREE THINGS I'M GRATEFUL FOR

I GIVE TODAY A

SOMETHING I WANT TO REMEMBER ABOUT TODAY

SOMETHING I COULD HAVE BEEN MORE GRATEFUL FOR TODAY

MY INTENTION FOR TOMORROW

DAY 237

THREE THINGS I'M GRATEFUL FOR

SOMETHING I WANT TO REMEMBER ABOUT TODAY

I GIVE TODAY A

MY INTENTION FOR
TOMORROW

SOMETHING I COULD HAVE BEEN MORE GRATEFUL FOR TODAY

DAY 238

DAY MONTH YEAR

THREE THINGS I'M GRATEFUL FOR

I GIVE TODAY A

SOMETHING I WANT TO REMEMBER ABOUT TODAY

SOMETHING I COULD HAVE BEEN MORE GRATEFUL FOR TODAY

MY INTENTION FOR TOMORROW

SOMETHING I COULD HAVE BEEN MORE GRATEFUL FOR THIS WEEK

I GIVE THIS WEEK A

SOMETHING I WANT TO REMEMBER ABOUT THIS WEEK

MY INTENTION FOR NEXT WEEK

SOMEONE I COULD HAVE FELT MORE GRATEFUL FOR THIS WEEK

DAY 239

DAY   MONTH   YEAR

THREE THINGS I'M GRATEFUL FOR

I GIVE TODAY A

SOMETHING I WANT TO REMEMBER ABOUT TODAY

SOMETHING I COULD HAVE BEEN MORE GRATEFUL FOR TODAY

MY INTENTION FOR
TOMORROW

DAY   MONTH   YEAR

THREE THINGS I'M GRATEFUL FOR

SOMETHING I WANT TO REMEMBER ABOUT TODAY   I GIVE TODAY A

MY INTENTION FOR
TOMORROW   SOMETHING I COULD HAVE BEEN MORE GRATEFUL FOR TODAY

DAY   MONTH   YEAR

THREE THINGS I'M GRATEFUL FOR

I GIVE TODAY A

SOMETHING I WANT TO REMEMBER ABOUT TODAY

SOMETHING I COULD HAVE BEEN MORE GRATEFUL FOR TODAY

MY INTENTION FOR TOMORROW

• • • • • • • • • • • • # DAY 242 • • • • • • • • • •

DAY   MONTH   YEAR

THREE THINGS I'M GRATEFUL FOR

SOMETHING I WANT TO REMEMBER ABOUT TODAY   I GIVE TODAY A

MY INTENTION FOR   SOMETHING I COULD HAVE BEEN MORE GRATEFUL FOR TODAY
TOMORROW

········· DAY 243 ·········

DAY MONTH YEAR

THREE THINGS I'M GRATEFUL FOR

I GIVE TODAY A

SOMETHING I WANT TO REMEMBER ABOUT TODAY

SOMETHING I COULD HAVE BEEN MORE GRATEFUL FOR TODAY

MY INTENTION FOR
TOMORROW

DAY   MONTH   YEAR

THREE THINGS I'M GRATEFUL FOR

SOMETHING I WANT TO REMEMBER ABOUT TODAY

I GIVE TODAY A

MY INTENTION FOR
TOMORROW

SOMETHING I COULD HAVE BEEN MORE GRATEFUL FOR TODAY

DAY 245

DAY   MONTH   YEAR

THREE THINGS I'M GRATEFUL FOR

I GIVE TODAY A

SOMETHING I WANT TO REMEMBER ABOUT TODAY

SOMETHING I COULD HAVE BEEN MORE GRATEFUL FOR TODAY

MY INTENTION FOR TOMORROW

PRACTICING GRATITUDE IS HOW WE ACKNOWLEDGE THAT THERE'S ENOUGH AND WE'RE ENOUGH.

BRENÉ BROWN

SOMETHING I COULD HAVE BEEN MORE GRATEFUL FOR THIS WEEK

I GIVE THIS WEEK A

SOMETHING I WANT TO REMEMBER ABOUT THIS WEEK

MY INTENTION FOR NEXT WEEK

SOMEONE I COULD HAVE FELT MORE GRATEFUL FOR THIS WEEK

DAY MONTH YEAR

THREE THINGS I'M GRATEFUL FOR

I GIVE TODAY A

SOMETHING I WANT TO REMEMBER ABOUT TODAY

SOMETHING I COULD HAVE BEEN MORE GRATEFUL FOR TODAY

MY INTENTION FOR TOMORROW

DAY 247

THREE THINGS I'M GRATEFUL FOR

SOMETHING I WANT TO REMEMBER ABOUT TODAY

I GIVE TODAY A

MY INTENTION FOR TOMORROW

SOMETHING I COULD HAVE BEEN MORE GRATEFUL FOR TODAY

DAY 248

DAY   MONTH   YEAR

THREE THINGS I'M GRATEFUL FOR

I GIVE TODAY A

SOMETHING I WANT TO REMEMBER ABOUT TODAY

SOMETHING I COULD HAVE BEEN MORE GRATEFUL FOR TODAY

MY INTENTION FOR
TOMORROW

DAY 249

DAY   MONTH   YEAR

THREE THINGS I'M GRATEFUL FOR

SOMETHING I WANT TO REMEMBER ABOUT TODAY   I GIVE TODAY A

MY INTENTION FOR
TOMORROW   SOMETHING I COULD HAVE BEEN MORE GRATEFUL FOR TODAY

DAY 250

THREE THINGS I'M GRATEFUL FOR

I GIVE TODAY A

SOMETHING I WANT TO REMEMBER ABOUT TODAY

SOMETHING I COULD HAVE BEEN MORE GRATEFUL FOR TODAY

MY INTENTION FOR TOMORROW

DAY 251

THREE THINGS I'M GRATEFUL FOR

SOMETHING I WANT TO REMEMBER ABOUT TODAY

I GIVE TODAY A

MY INTENTION FOR
TOMORROW

SOMETHING I COULD HAVE BEEN MORE GRATEFUL FOR TODAY

DAY 252

DAY   MONTH   YEAR

THREE THINGS I'M GRATEFUL FOR

I GIVE TODAY A

SOMETHING I WANT TO REMEMBER ABOUT TODAY

SOMETHING I COULD HAVE BEEN MORE GRATEFUL FOR TODAY

MY INTENTION FOR TOMORROW

DAY 252

WEAR GRATITUDE LIKE A CLOAK AND IT WILL FEED
EVERY CORNER OF YOUR LIFE.

RUMI

SOMETHING I COULD HAVE BEEN MORE GRATEFUL FOR THESE
PAST FOUR WEEKS

I GIVE THE PAST FOUR WEEKS A

SOMETHING I WANT TO REMEMBER ABOUT THE PAST FOUR WEEKS

MY INTENTION FOR THE
NEXT FOUR WEEKS

SOMEONE I COULD HAVE FELT MORE GRATEFUL FOR THESE PAST
FOUR WEEKS

DAY 253

DAY MONTH YEAR

THREE THINGS I'M GRATEFUL FOR

I GIVE TODAY A

SOMETHING I WANT TO REMEMBER ABOUT TODAY

SOMETHING I COULD HAVE BEEN MORE GRATEFUL FOR TODAY

MY INTENTION FOR TOMORROW

DAY 254

DAY   MONTH   YEAR

THREE THINGS I'M GRATEFUL FOR

SOMETHING I WANT TO REMEMBER ABOUT TODAY

I GIVE TODAY A

MY INTENTION FOR
TOMORROW

SOMETHING I COULD HAVE BEEN MORE GRATEFUL FOR TODAY

DAY 255

DAY   MONTH   YEAR

THREE THINGS I'M GRATEFUL FOR

I GIVE TODAY A

SOMETHING I WANT TO REMEMBER ABOUT TODAY

SOMETHING I COULD HAVE BEEN MORE GRATEFUL FOR TODAY

MY INTENTION FOR TOMORROW

DAY 256

Three things I'm grateful for

Something I want to remember about today

I give today a

My intention for
tomorrow

Something I could have been more grateful for today

DAY 257

DAY   MONTH   YEAR

THREE THINGS I'M GRATEFUL FOR

I GIVE TODAY A

SOMETHING I WANT TO REMEMBER ABOUT TODAY

SOMETHING I COULD HAVE BEEN MORE GRATEFUL FOR TODAY

MY INTENTION FOR TOMORROW

DAY   MONTH   YEAR

THREE THINGS I'M GRATEFUL FOR

SOMETHING I WANT TO REMEMBER ABOUT TODAY

I GIVE TODAY A

MY INTENTION FOR
TOMORROW

SOMETHING I COULD HAVE BEEN MORE GRATEFUL FOR TODAY

DAY   MONTH   YEAR

THREE THINGS I'M GRATEFUL FOR

I GIVE TODAY A

SOMETHING I WANT TO REMEMBER ABOUT TODAY

SOMETHING I COULD HAVE BEEN MORE GRATEFUL FOR TODAY

MY INTENTION FOR TOMORROW

DAY 259

GRATITUDE IS THE HEALTHIEST OF ALL HUMAN EMOTIONS. THE MORE YOU EXPRESS GRATITUDE FOR WHAT YOU HAVE, THE MORE LIKELY YOU WILL HAVE EVEN MORE TO EXPRESS GRATITUDE FOR.
ZIG ZIGLAR

SOMETHING I COULD HAVE BEEN MORE GRATEFUL FOR THIS WEEK

I GIVE THIS WEEK A

SOMETHING I WANT TO REMEMBER ABOUT THIS WEEK

MY INTENTION FOR NEXT WEEK

SOMEONE I COULD HAVE FELT MORE GRATEFUL FOR THIS WEEK

Day 260

Day Month Year

Three things I'm grateful for

I give today a

Something I want to remember about today

Something I could have been more grateful for today

My intention for tomorrow

DAY 261

DAY   MONTH   YEAR

THREE THINGS I'M GRATEFUL FOR

SOMETHING I WANT TO REMEMBER ABOUT TODAY

I GIVE TODAY A

MY INTENTION FOR TOMORROW

SOMETHING I COULD HAVE BEEN MORE GRATEFUL FOR TODAY

DAY 262

THREE THINGS I'M GRATEFUL FOR

I GIVE TODAY A

SOMETHING I WANT TO REMEMBER ABOUT TODAY

SOMETHING I COULD HAVE BEEN MORE GRATEFUL FOR TODAY

MY INTENTION FOR
TOMORROW

DAY 263

DAY   MONTH   YEAR

THREE THINGS I'M GRATEFUL FOR

SOMETHING I WANT TO REMEMBER ABOUT TODAY

I GIVE TODAY A

MY INTENTION FOR TOMORROW

SOMETHING I COULD HAVE BEEN MORE GRATEFUL FOR TODAY

DAY 264

DAY	MONTH	YEAR

THREE THINGS I'M GRATEFUL FOR

I GIVE TODAY A

SOMETHING I WANT TO REMEMBER ABOUT TODAY

SOMETHING I COULD HAVE BEEN MORE GRATEFUL FOR TODAY

MY INTENTION FOR TOMORROW

DAY 265

DAY   MONTH   YEAR

THREE THINGS I'M GRATEFUL FOR

SOMETHING I WANT TO REMEMBER ABOUT TODAY   I GIVE TODAY A

MY INTENTION FOR   SOMETHING I COULD HAVE BEEN MORE GRATEFUL FOR TODAY
TOMORROW

DAY 266

DAY   MONTH   YEAR

THREE THINGS I'M GRATEFUL FOR

I GIVE TODAY A

SOMETHING I WANT TO REMEMBER ABOUT TODAY

SOMETHING I COULD HAVE BEEN MORE GRATEFUL FOR TODAY

MY INTENTION FOR TOMORROW

DAY 266

IF YOU CAN'T BE CONTENT WITH WHAT YOU HAVE RECEIVED, BE THANKFUL FOR WHAT YOU HAVE ESCAPED.

UNKNOWN

SOMETHING I COULD HAVE BEEN MORE GRATEFUL FOR THIS WEEK

I GIVE THIS WEEK A

SOMETHING I WANT TO REMEMBER ABOUT THIS WEEK

MY INTENTION FOR NEXT WEEK

SOMEONE I COULD HAVE FELT MORE GRATEFUL FOR THIS WEEK

DAY   MONTH   YEAR

Three things I'm grateful for

I GIVE TODAY A

SOMETHING I WANT TO REMEMBER ABOUT TODAY

SOMETHING I COULD HAVE BEEN MORE GRATEFUL FOR TODAY

MY INTENTION FOR TOMORROW

DAY   MONTH   YEAR

THREE THINGS I'M GRATEFUL FOR

SOMETHING I WANT TO REMEMBER ABOUT TODAY

I GIVE TODAY A

MY INTENTION FOR TOMORROW

SOMETHING I COULD HAVE BEEN MORE GRATEFUL FOR TODAY

DAY   MONTH   YEAR

THREE THINGS I'M GRATEFUL FOR

I GIVE TODAY A

SOMETHING I WANT TO REMEMBER ABOUT TODAY

SOMETHING I COULD HAVE BEEN MORE GRATEFUL FOR TODAY

MY INTENTION FOR TOMORROW

DAY   MONTH   YEAR

THREE THINGS I'M GRATEFUL FOR

SOMETHING I WANT TO REMEMBER ABOUT TODAY   I GIVE TODAY A

MY INTENTION FOR
TOMORROW   SOMETHING I COULD HAVE BEEN MORE GRATEFUL FOR TODAY

DAY   MONTH   YEAR

THREE THINGS I'M GRATEFUL FOR

I GIVE TODAY A

SOMETHING I WANT TO REMEMBER ABOUT TODAY

SOMETHING I COULD HAVE BEEN MORE GRATEFUL FOR TODAY

MY INTENTION FOR TOMORROW

DAY   MONTH   YEAR

THREE THINGS I'M GRATEFUL FOR

SOMETHING I WANT TO REMEMBER ABOUT TODAY   I GIVE TODAY A

MY INTENTION FOR   SOMETHING I COULD HAVE BEEN MORE GRATEFUL FOR TODAY
TOMORROW

DAY 273

DAY   MONTH   YEAR

THREE THINGS I'M GRATEFUL FOR

I GIVE TODAY A

SOMETHING I WANT TO REMEMBER ABOUT TODAY

SOMETHING I COULD HAVE BEEN MORE GRATEFUL FOR TODAY

MY INTENTION FOR
TOMORROW

WK 39

GRATITUDE CAN TRANSFORM COMMON DAYS INTO THANKSGIVINGS, TURN ROUTINE JOBS INTO JOY, AND CHANGE ORDINARY OPPORTUNITIES INTO BLESSINGS.

WILLIAM ARTHUR WARD

SOMETHING I COULD HAVE BEEN MORE GRATEFUL FOR THIS WEEK

I GIVE THIS WEEK A

SOMETHING I WANT TO REMEMBER ABOUT THIS WEEK

MY INTENTION FOR NEXT WEEK

SOMEONE I COULD HAVE FELT MORE GRATEFUL FOR THIS WEEK

9 MONTHS

Let's do some more reflecting. Run through the past thirteen weeks and answer the following:

SOMETHING I WANT TO REMEMBER ABOUT THE PAST THREE MONTHS

LOOKING BACK OVER THE PAST THREE MONTHS, I AM MOST GRATEFUL FOR

THE BIGGEST LESSON I LEARNED OVER THE PAST THREE MONTHS

SOMEONE OR SOMETHING I COULD HAVE FELT MORE GRATEFUL FOR DURING THE PAST THREE MONTHS

I GIVE THE PAST THREE MONTHS A

WHAT HAVE I BEEN UNABLE TO FEEL GRATEFUL FOR DURING THE PAST THREE MONTHS? CAN I REFORMULATE THAT THOUGHT ANYWAY?

I AM GRATEFUL....

WHEN LOOKING BACK ON HOW I'VE RATED MY WEEKS THUS FAR, THE NUMBERS TELL ME

MY INTENTION FOR THE NEXT THREE MONTHS

WHO HAVE I BEEN UNABLE TO FEEL GRATEFUL FOR DURING THE PAST THREE MONTHS? CAN I REFORMULATE THAT THOUGHT ANYWAY? I AM GRATEFUL....

DAY 274

DAY   MONTH   YEAR

THREE THINGS I'M GRATEFUL FOR

I GIVE TODAY A

SOMETHING I WANT TO REMEMBER ABOUT TODAY

SOMETHING I COULD HAVE BEEN MORE GRATEFUL FOR TODAY

MY INTENTION FOR
TOMORROW

DAY 275

<table>
<tr><td>DAY</td><td>MONTH</td><td>YEAR</td></tr>
</table>

THREE THINGS I'M GRATEFUL FOR

SOMETHING I WANT TO REMEMBER ABOUT TODAY

I GIVE TODAY A

MY INTENTION FOR TOMORROW

SOMETHING I COULD HAVE BEEN MORE GRATEFUL FOR TODAY

DAY 276

DAY   MONTH   YEAR

THREE THINGS I'M GRATEFUL FOR

I GIVE TODAY A

SOMETHING I WANT TO REMEMBER ABOUT TODAY

SOMETHING I COULD HAVE BEEN MORE GRATEFUL FOR TODAY

MY INTENTION FOR TOMORROW

DAY 277

DAY   MONTH   YEAR

THREE THINGS I'M GRATEFUL FOR

SOMETHING I WANT TO REMEMBER ABOUT TODAY   I GIVE TODAY A

MY INTENTION FOR   SOMETHING I COULD HAVE BEEN MORE GRATEFUL FOR TODAY
TOMORROW

DAY 278

DAY   MONTH   YEAR

THREE THINGS I'M GRATEFUL FOR

I GIVE TODAY A

SOMETHING I WANT TO REMEMBER ABOUT TODAY

SOMETHING I COULD HAVE BEEN MORE GRATEFUL FOR TODAY

MY INTENTION FOR
TOMORROW

DAY 279

THREE THINGS I'M GRATEFUL FOR

SOMETHING I WANT TO REMEMBER ABOUT TODAY

I GIVE TODAY A

MY INTENTION FOR TOMORROW

SOMETHING I COULD HAVE BEEN MORE GRATEFUL FOR TODAY

DAY 280

DAY   MONTH   YEAR

THREE THINGS I'M GRATEFUL FOR

I GIVE TODAY A   SOMETHING I WANT TO REMEMBER ABOUT TODAY

SOMETHING I COULD HAVE BEEN MORE GRATEFUL FOR TODAY   MY INTENTION FOR TOMORROW

DAY 280

THE MORE YOU PRAISE AND CELEBRATE YOUR LIFE, THE
MORE THERE IS IN LIFE TO CELEBRATE.

OPRAH WINFREY

SOMETHING I COULD HAVE BEEN MORE GRATEFUL FOR THESE
PAST FOUR WEEKS

I GIVE THE PAST FOUR WEEKS A

SOMETHING I WANT TO REMEMBER ABOUT THE PAST FOUR WEEKS

MY INTENTION FOR THE
NEXT FOUR WEEKS

SOMEONE I COULD HAVE FELT MORE GRATEFUL FOR THESE PAST
FOUR WEEKS

DAY 281

DAY   MONTH   YEAR

THREE THINGS I'M GRATEFUL FOR

I GIVE TODAY A

SOMETHING I WANT TO REMEMBER ABOUT TODAY

SOMETHING I COULD HAVE BEEN MORE GRATEFUL FOR TODAY

MY INTENTION FOR TOMORROW

DAY 282

DAY   MONTH   YEAR

THREE THINGS I'M GRATEFUL FOR

SOMETHING I WANT TO REMEMBER ABOUT TODAY   I GIVE TODAY A

MY INTENTION FOR TOMORROW   SOMETHING I COULD HAVE BEEN MORE GRATEFUL FOR TODAY

DAY 283

DAY	MONTH	YEAR

THREE THINGS I'M GRATEFUL FOR

I GIVE TODAY A

SOMETHING I WANT TO REMEMBER ABOUT TODAY

SOMETHING I COULD HAVE BEEN MORE GRATEFUL FOR TODAY

MY INTENTION FOR TOMORROW

DAY   MONTH   YEAR

THREE THINGS I'M GRATEFUL FOR

SOMETHING I WANT TO REMEMBER ABOUT TODAY

I GIVE TODAY A

MY INTENTION FOR
TOMORROW

SOMETHING I COULD HAVE BEEN MORE GRATEFUL FOR TODAY

DAY   MONTH   YEAR

THREE THINGS I'M GRATEFUL FOR

I GIVE TODAY A

SOMETHING I WANT TO REMEMBER ABOUT TODAY

SOMETHING I COULD HAVE BEEN MORE GRATEFUL FOR TODAY

MY INTENTION FOR
TOMORROW

DAY 286

THREE THINGS I'M GRATEFUL FOR

SOMETHING I WANT TO REMEMBER ABOUT TODAY

I GIVE TODAY A

MY INTENTION FOR
TOMORROW

SOMETHING I COULD HAVE BEEN MORE GRATEFUL FOR TODAY

Day 287

Day   Month   Year

Three things I'm grateful for

I give today a

Something I want to remember about today

Something I could have been more grateful for today

My intention for tomorrow

DAY 287

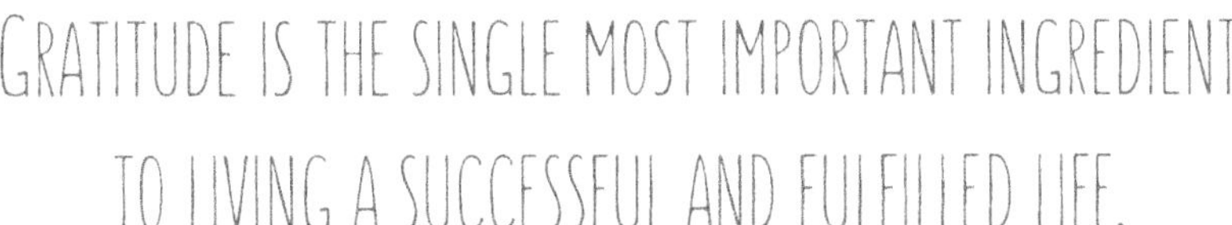

GRATITUDE IS THE SINGLE MOST IMPORTANT INGREDIENT
TO LIVING A SUCCESSFUL AND FULFILLED LIFE.

JACK CANFIELD

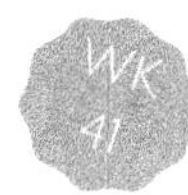

SOMETHING I COULD HAVE BEEN MORE GRATEFUL FOR THIS WEEK

I GIVE THIS WEEK A

SOMETHING I WANT TO REMEMBER ABOUT THIS WEEK

MY INTENTION FOR NEXT
WEEK

SOMEONE I COULD HAVE FELT MORE GRATEFUL FOR THIS WEEK

DAY 288

DAY   MONTH   YEAR

THREE THINGS I'M GRATEFUL FOR

I GIVE TODAY A

SOMETHING I WANT TO REMEMBER ABOUT TODAY

SOMETHING I COULD HAVE BEEN MORE GRATEFUL FOR TODAY

MY INTENTION FOR TOMORROW

DAY 289

DAY   MONTH   YEAR

THREE THINGS I'M GRATEFUL FOR

SOMETHING I WANT TO REMEMBER ABOUT TODAY   I GIVE TODAY A

MY INTENTION FOR   SOMETHING I COULD HAVE BEEN MORE GRATEFUL FOR TODAY
TOMORROW

Day 290

Day   Month   Year

Three things I'm grateful for

I give today a

Something I want to remember about today

Something I could have been more grateful for today

My intention for tomorrow

DAY 291

Day   Month   Year

Three things I'm grateful for

Something I want to remember about today

I give today a

My intention for
tomorrow

Something I could have been more grateful for today

DAY 292

THREE THINGS I'M GRATEFUL FOR

I GIVE TODAY A

SOMETHING I WANT TO REMEMBER ABOUT TODAY

SOMETHING I COULD HAVE BEEN MORE GRATEFUL FOR TODAY

MY INTENTION FOR
TOMORROW

DAY 293

Three things I'm grateful for

Something I want to remember about today

I give today a

My intention for
tomorrow

Something I could have been more grateful for today

DAY 294

DAY   MONTH   YEAR

THREE THINGS I'M GRATEFUL FOR

I GIVE TODAY A

SOMETHING I WANT TO REMEMBER ABOUT TODAY

SOMETHING I COULD HAVE BEEN MORE GRATEFUL FOR TODAY

MY INTENTION FOR TOMORROW

WK
42

This is a wonderful day. I've never seen this one before.

Maya Angelou

Something I could have been more grateful for this week

I give this week a

Something I want to remember about this week

My intention for next week

Someone I could have felt more grateful for this week

DAY   MONTH   YEAR

THREE THINGS I'M GRATEFUL FOR

I GIVE TODAY A

SOMETHING I WANT TO REMEMBER ABOUT TODAY

SOMETHING I COULD HAVE BEEN MORE GRATEFUL FOR TODAY

MY INTENTION FOR TOMORROW

DAY   MONTH   YEAR

THREE THINGS I'M GRATEFUL FOR

SOMETHING I WANT TO REMEMBER ABOUT TODAY

I GIVE TODAY A

MY INTENTION FOR
TOMORROW

SOMETHING I COULD HAVE BEEN MORE GRATEFUL FOR TODAY

DAY   MONTH   YEAR

THREE THINGS I'M GRATEFUL FOR

I GIVE TODAY A

SOMETHING I WANT TO REMEMBER ABOUT TODAY

SOMETHING I COULD HAVE BEEN MORE GRATEFUL FOR TODAY

MY INTENTION FOR TOMORROW

DAY   MONTH   YEAR

THREE THINGS I'M GRATEFUL FOR

SOMETHING I WANT TO REMEMBER ABOUT TODAY   I GIVE TODAY A

MY INTENTION FOR   SOMETHING I COULD HAVE BEEN MORE GRATEFUL FOR TODAY
TOMORROW

DAY   MONTH   YEAR

THREE THINGS I'M GRATEFUL FOR

I GIVE TODAY A

SOMETHING I WANT TO REMEMBER ABOUT TODAY

SOMETHING I COULD HAVE BEEN MORE GRATEFUL FOR TODAY

MY INTENTION FOR
TOMORROW

Day 300

Three things I'm grateful for

Something I want to remember about today

I give today a

My intention for tomorrow

Something I could have been more grateful for today

DAY   MONTH   YEAR

THREE THINGS I'M GRATEFUL FOR

I GIVE TODAY A

SOMETHING I WANT TO REMEMBER ABOUT TODAY

SOMETHING I COULD HAVE BEEN MORE GRATEFUL FOR TODAY

MY INTENTION FOR TOMORROW

WE FORGET THAT WAKING UP EACH DAY IS THE FIRST THING WE SHOULD BE GRATEFUL FOR.

UNKNOWN

SOMETHING I COULD HAVE BEEN MORE GRATEFUL FOR THIS WEEK

I GIVE THIS WEEK A

SOMETHING I WANT TO REMEMBER ABOUT THIS WEEK

MY INTENTION FOR NEXT
WEEK

SOMEONE I COULD HAVE FELT MORE GRATEFUL FOR THIS WEEK

DAY 302

DAY   MONTH   YEAR

THREE THINGS I'M GRATEFUL FOR

I GIVE TODAY A

SOMETHING I WANT TO REMEMBER ABOUT TODAY

SOMETHING I COULD HAVE BEEN MORE GRATEFUL FOR TODAY

MY INTENTION FOR
TOMORROW

DAY 303

THREE THINGS I'M GRATEFUL FOR

SOMETHING I WANT TO REMEMBER ABOUT TODAY

I GIVE TODAY A

MY INTENTION FOR
TOMORROW

SOMETHING I COULD HAVE BEEN MORE GRATEFUL FOR TODAY

DAY 304

DAY   MONTH   YEAR

THREE THINGS I'M GRATEFUL FOR

I GIVE TODAY A

SOMETHING I WANT TO REMEMBER ABOUT TODAY

SOMETHING I COULD HAVE BEEN MORE GRATEFUL FOR TODAY

MY INTENTION FOR TOMORROW

DAY 305

THREE THINGS I'M GRATEFUL FOR

SOMETHING I WANT TO REMEMBER ABOUT TODAY

I GIVE TODAY A

MY INTENTION FOR
TOMORROW

SOMETHING I COULD HAVE BEEN MORE GRATEFUL FOR TODAY

DAY 306

DAY   MONTH   YEAR

THREE THINGS I'M GRATEFUL FOR

I GIVE TODAY A

SOMETHING I WANT TO REMEMBER ABOUT TODAY

SOMETHING I COULD HAVE BEEN MORE GRATEFUL FOR TODAY

MY INTENTION FOR
TOMORROW

DAY 307

Day   Month   Year

Three things I'm grateful for

Something I want to remember about today   I give today a

My intention for tomorrow   Something I could have been more grateful for today

DAY 308

DAY   MONTH   YEAR

THREE THINGS I'M GRATEFUL FOR

I GIVE TODAY A

SOMETHING I WANT TO REMEMBER ABOUT TODAY

SOMETHING I COULD HAVE BEEN MORE GRATEFUL FOR TODAY

MY INTENTION FOR
TOMORROW

DAY 308

WHEN GRATITUDE BECOMES YOUR DEFAULT SETTING, LIFE CHANGES.

Nancy Leigh DeMoss

SOMETHING I COULD HAVE BEEN MORE GRATEFUL FOR THESE PAST FOUR WEEKS

I GIVE THE PAST FOUR WEEKS A

SOMETHING I WANT TO REMEMBER ABOUT THE PAST FOUR WEEKS

MY INTENTION FOR THE NEXT FOUR WEEKS

SOMEONE I COULD HAVE FELT MORE GRATEFUL FOR THESE PAST FOUR WEEKS

DAY 309

DAY MONTH YEAR

THREE THINGS I'M GRATEFUL FOR

I GIVE TODAY A

SOMETHING I WANT TO REMEMBER ABOUT TODAY

SOMETHING I COULD HAVE BEEN MORE GRATEFUL FOR TODAY

MY INTENTION FOR TOMORROW

DAY   MONTH   YEAR

THREE THINGS I'M GRATEFUL FOR

SOMETHING I WANT TO REMEMBER ABOUT TODAY

I GIVE TODAY A

MY INTENTION FOR
TOMORROW

SOMETHING I COULD HAVE BEEN MORE GRATEFUL FOR TODAY

DAY 311

DAY   MONTH   YEAR

THREE THINGS I'M GRATEFUL FOR

I GIVE TODAY A

SOMETHING I WANT TO REMEMBER ABOUT TODAY

SOMETHING I COULD HAVE BEEN MORE GRATEFUL FOR TODAY

MY INTENTION FOR TOMORROW

DAY 312

DAY   MONTH   YEAR

THREE THINGS I'M GRATEFUL FOR

SOMETHING I WANT TO REMEMBER ABOUT TODAY   I GIVE TODAY A

MY INTENTION FOR
TOMORROW   SOMETHING I COULD HAVE BEEN MORE GRATEFUL FOR TODAY

DAY 313

DAY   MONTH   YEAR

THREE THINGS I'M GRATEFUL FOR

I GIVE TODAY A

SOMETHING I WANT TO REMEMBER ABOUT TODAY

SOMETHING I COULD HAVE BEEN MORE GRATEFUL FOR TODAY

MY INTENTION FOR TOMORROW

DAY 314

Day   Month   Year

Three things I'm grateful for

Something I want to remember about today

I give today a

My intention for
tomorrow

Something I could have been more grateful for today

DAY 315

<table>
<tr><td>Day</td><td>Month</td><td>Year</td></tr>
</table>

Three things I'm grateful for

I give today a

Something I want to remember about today

Something I could have been more grateful for today

My intention for tomorrow

DAY 315

IF YOU WANT TO FIND HAPPINESS, FIND GRATITUDE.

STEVE MARABOLI

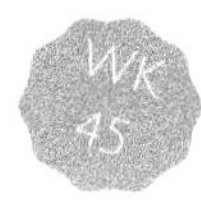

SOMETHING I COULD HAVE BEEN MORE GRATEFUL FOR THIS WEEK

I GIVE THIS WEEK A

SOMETHING I WANT TO REMEMBER ABOUT THIS WEEK

MY INTENTION FOR NEXT WEEK

SOMEONE I COULD HAVE FELT MORE GRATEFUL FOR THIS WEEK

DAY 316

DAY   MONTH   YEAR

THREE THINGS I'M GRATEFUL FOR

I GIVE TODAY A

SOMETHING I WANT TO REMEMBER ABOUT TODAY

SOMETHING I COULD HAVE BEEN MORE GRATEFUL FOR TODAY

MY INTENTION FOR TOMORROW

DAY 317

THREE THINGS I'M GRATEFUL FOR

SOMETHING I WANT TO REMEMBER ABOUT TODAY

I GIVE TODAY A

MY INTENTION FOR
TOMORROW

SOMETHING I COULD HAVE BEEN MORE GRATEFUL FOR TODAY

DAY 318

DAY   MONTH   YEAR

THREE THINGS I'M GRATEFUL FOR

I GIVE TODAY A

SOMETHING I WANT TO REMEMBER ABOUT TODAY

SOMETHING I COULD HAVE BEEN MORE GRATEFUL FOR TODAY

MY INTENTION FOR TOMORROW

DAY 319

THREE THINGS I'M GRATEFUL FOR

SOMETHING I WANT TO REMEMBER ABOUT TODAY

I GIVE TODAY A

MY INTENTION FOR TOMORROW

SOMETHING I COULD HAVE BEEN MORE GRATEFUL FOR TODAY

DAY 320

DAY   MONTH   YEAR

THREE THINGS I'M GRATEFUL FOR

I GIVE TODAY A

SOMETHING I WANT TO REMEMBER ABOUT TODAY

SOMETHING I COULD HAVE BEEN MORE GRATEFUL FOR TODAY

MY INTENTION FOR
TOMORROW

DAY 321

THREE THINGS I'M GRATEFUL FOR

SOMETHING I WANT TO REMEMBER ABOUT TODAY

I GIVE TODAY A

MY INTENTION FOR
TOMORROW

SOMETHING I COULD HAVE BEEN MORE GRATEFUL FOR TODAY

DAY 322

DAY   MONTH   YEAR

THREE THINGS I'M GRATEFUL FOR

I GIVE TODAY A

SOMETHING I WANT TO REMEMBER ABOUT TODAY

SOMETHING I COULD HAVE BEEN MORE GRATEFUL FOR TODAY

MY INTENTION FOR TOMORROW

DAY 322

HAPPINESS CANNOT BE TRAVELED TO, OWNED, EARNED, WORN OR CONSUMED. HAPPINESS IS THE SPIRITUAL EXPERIENCE OF LIVING EVERY MINUTE WITH LOVE, GRACE AND GRATITUDE.
Denis Waitley

SOMETHING I COULD HAVE BEEN MORE GRATEFUL FOR THIS WEEK

I GIVE THIS WEEK A

SOMETHING I WANT TO REMEMBER ABOUT THIS WEEK

MY INTENTION FOR NEXT WEEK

SOMEONE I COULD HAVE FELT MORE GRATEFUL FOR THIS WEEK

DAY   MONTH   YEAR

THREE THINGS I'M GRATEFUL FOR

I GIVE TODAY A

SOMETHING I WANT TO REMEMBER ABOUT TODAY

SOMETHING I COULD HAVE BEEN MORE GRATEFUL FOR TODAY

MY INTENTION FOR
TOMORROW

DAY   MONTH   YEAR

Three things I'm grateful for

Something I want to remember about today

I give today a

My intention for
tomorrow

Something I could have been more grateful for today

DAY 325

DAY   MONTH   YEAR

THREE THINGS I'M GRATEFUL FOR

I GIVE TODAY A

SOMETHING I WANT TO REMEMBER ABOUT TODAY

SOMETHING I COULD HAVE BEEN MORE GRATEFUL FOR TODAY

MY INTENTION FOR
TOMORROW

DAY   MONTH   YEAR

THREE THINGS I'M GRATEFUL FOR

SOMETHING I WANT TO REMEMBER ABOUT TODAY   I GIVE TODAY A

MY INTENTION FOR
TOMORROW   SOMETHING I COULD HAVE BEEN MORE GRATEFUL FOR TODAY

DAY   MONTH   YEAR

THREE THINGS I'M GRATEFUL FOR

I GIVE TODAY A

SOMETHING I WANT TO REMEMBER ABOUT TODAY

SOMETHING I COULD HAVE BEEN MORE GRATEFUL FOR TODAY

MY INTENTION FOR
TOMORROW

DAY 328

THREE THINGS I'M GRATEFUL FOR

SOMETHING I WANT TO REMEMBER ABOUT TODAY

I GIVE TODAY A

MY INTENTION FOR TOMORROW

SOMETHING I COULD HAVE BEEN MORE GRATEFUL FOR TODAY

DAY   MONTH   YEAR

THREE THINGS I'M GRATEFUL FOR

I GIVE TODAY A

SOMETHING I WANT TO REMEMBER ABOUT TODAY

SOMETHING I COULD HAVE BEEN MORE GRATEFUL FOR TODAY

MY INTENTION FOR
TOMORROW

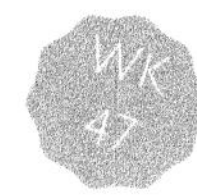

THE MOST POWERFUL WEAPON AGAINST YOUR DAILY BATTLES IS FINDING THE COURAGE TO BE GRATEFUL ANYWAY.

UNKNOWN

SOMETHING I COULD HAVE BEEN MORE GRATEFUL FOR THIS WEEK

I GIVE THIS WEEK A

SOMETHING I WANT TO REMEMBER ABOUT THIS WEEK

MY INTENTION FOR NEXT WEEK

SOMEONE I COULD HAVE FELT MORE GRATEFUL FOR THIS WEEK

DAY 330

DAY   MONTH   YEAR

THREE THINGS I'M GRATEFUL FOR

I GIVE TODAY A

SOMETHING I WANT TO REMEMBER ABOUT TODAY

SOMETHING I COULD HAVE BEEN MORE GRATEFUL FOR TODAY

MY INTENTION FOR TOMORROW

DAY 331

Day   Month   Year

Three things I'm grateful for

Something I want to remember about today

I give today a

My intention for
tomorrow

Something I could have been more grateful for today

DAY 332

DAY MONTH YEAR

THREE THINGS I'M GRATEFUL FOR

I GIVE TODAY A

SOMETHING I WANT TO REMEMBER ABOUT TODAY

SOMETHING I COULD HAVE BEEN MORE GRATEFUL FOR TODAY

MY INTENTION FOR TOMORROW

DAY 333

DAY   MONTH   YEAR

THREE THINGS I'M GRATEFUL FOR

SOMETHING I WANT TO REMEMBER ABOUT TODAY

I GIVE TODAY A

MY INTENTION FOR
TOMORROW

SOMETHING I COULD HAVE BEEN MORE GRATEFUL FOR TODAY

DAY 334

DAY   MONTH   YEAR

THREE THINGS I'M GRATEFUL FOR

I GIVE TODAY A

SOMETHING I WANT TO REMEMBER ABOUT TODAY

SOMETHING I COULD HAVE BEEN MORE GRATEFUL FOR TODAY

MY INTENTION FOR TOMORROW

DAY 335

THREE THINGS I'M GRATEFUL FOR

SOMETHING I WANT TO REMEMBER ABOUT TODAY

I GIVE TODAY A

MY INTENTION FOR
TOMORROW

SOMETHING I COULD HAVE BEEN MORE GRATEFUL FOR TODAY

DAY 336

Day   Month   Year

Three things I'm grateful for

I give today a

Something I want to remember about today

Something I could have been more grateful for today

My intention for tomorrow

 # DAY 336 

IF YOU ARE GRATEFUL FOR WHERE YOU ARE, YOU GOTTA RESPECT THE ROAD THAT GOT YOU THERE.

CLEO WADE

SOMETHING I COULD HAVE BEEN MORE GRATEFUL FOR THESE PAST FOUR WEEKS

I GIVE THE PAST FOUR WEEKS A

SOMETHING I WANT TO REMEMBER ABOUT THE PAST FOUR WEEKS

MY INTENTION FOR THE NEXT FOUR WEEKS

SOMEONE I COULD HAVE FELT MORE GRATEFUL FOR THESE PAST FOUR WEEKS

DAY 337

THREE THINGS I'M GRATEFUL FOR

I GIVE TODAY A

SOMETHING I WANT TO REMEMBER ABOUT TODAY

SOMETHING I COULD HAVE BEEN MORE GRATEFUL FOR TODAY

MY INTENTION FOR
TOMORROW

DAY 338

THREE THINGS I'M GRATEFUL FOR

SOMETHING I WANT TO REMEMBER ABOUT TODAY

I GIVE TODAY A

MY INTENTION FOR
TOMORROW

SOMETHING I COULD HAVE BEEN MORE GRATEFUL FOR TODAY

DAY 339

THREE THINGS I'M GRATEFUL FOR

I GIVE TODAY A

SOMETHING I WANT TO REMEMBER ABOUT TODAY

SOMETHING I COULD HAVE BEEN MORE GRATEFUL FOR TODAY

MY INTENTION FOR TOMORROW

Day 340

Day   Month   Year

Three things I'm grateful for

Something I want to remember about today

I give today a

My intention for
tomorrow

Something I could have been more grateful for today

DAY 341

DAY	MONTH	YEAR

THREE THINGS I'M GRATEFUL FOR

I GIVE TODAY A

SOMETHING I WANT TO REMEMBER ABOUT TODAY

SOMETHING I COULD HAVE BEEN MORE GRATEFUL FOR TODAY

MY INTENTION FOR TOMORROW

Day 342

Day   Month   Year

Three things I'm grateful for

Something I want to remember about today   I give today a

My intention for   Something I could have been more grateful for today
tomorrow

Day 343

Day   Month   Year

Three things I'm grateful for

I give today a

Something I want to remember about today

Something I could have been more grateful for today

My intention for tomorrow

DAY 343

WHAT SEPARATES PRIVILEGE FROM ENTITLEMENT
IS GRATITUDE.
BRENE BROWN

SOMETHING I COULD HAVE BEEN MORE GRATEFUL FOR THIS WEEK

I GIVE THIS WEEK A

SOMETHING I WANT TO REMEMBER ABOUT THIS WEEK

MY INTENTION FOR NEXT WEEK

SOMEONE I COULD HAVE FELT MORE GRATEFUL FOR THIS WEEK

DAY 344

DAY   MONTH   YEAR

THREE THINGS I'M GRATEFUL FOR

I GIVE TODAY A

SOMETHING I WANT TO REMEMBER ABOUT TODAY

SOMETHING I COULD HAVE BEEN MORE GRATEFUL FOR TODAY

MY INTENTION FOR TOMORROW

DAY 345

DAY   MONTH   YEAR

THREE THINGS I'M GRATEFUL FOR

SOMETHING I WANT TO REMEMBER ABOUT TODAY

I GIVE TODAY A

MY INTENTION FOR TOMORROW

SOMETHING I COULD HAVE BEEN MORE GRATEFUL FOR TODAY

DAY 346

DAY   MONTH   YEAR

THREE THINGS I'M GRATEFUL FOR

I GIVE TODAY A

SOMETHING I WANT TO REMEMBER ABOUT TODAY

SOMETHING I COULD HAVE BEEN MORE GRATEFUL FOR TODAY

MY INTENTION FOR TOMORROW

DAY 347

DAY   MONTH   YEAR

THREE THINGS I'M GRATEFUL FOR

SOMETHING I WANT TO REMEMBER ABOUT TODAY

I GIVE TODAY A

MY INTENTION FOR TOMORROW

SOMETHING I COULD HAVE BEEN MORE GRATEFUL FOR TODAY

DAY 348

DAY   MONTH   YEAR

THREE THINGS I'M GRATEFUL FOR

I GIVE TODAY A

SOMETHING I WANT TO REMEMBER ABOUT TODAY

SOMETHING I COULD HAVE BEEN MORE GRATEFUL FOR TODAY

MY INTENTION FOR TOMORROW

DAY   MONTH   YEAR

THREE THINGS I'M GRATEFUL FOR

SOMETHING I WANT TO REMEMBER ABOUT TODAY

I GIVE TODAY A

MY INTENTION FOR
TOMORROW

SOMETHING I COULD HAVE BEEN MORE GRATEFUL FOR TODAY

DAY 350

DAY   MONTH   YEAR

THREE THINGS I'M GRATEFUL FOR

I GIVE TODAY A

SOMETHING I WANT TO REMEMBER ABOUT TODAY

SOMETHING I COULD HAVE BEEN MORE GRATEFUL FOR TODAY

MY INTENTION FOR
TOMORROW

DAY 350

IT COSTS $0.00 TO BE GRATEFUL FOR
WHAT YOU ALREADY HAVE.

UNKNOWN

SOMETHING I COULD HAVE BEEN MORE GRATEFUL FOR THIS WEEK

I GIVE THIS WEEK A

SOMETHING I WANT TO REMEMBER ABOUT THIS WEEK

MY INTENTION FOR NEXT WEEK

SOMEONE I COULD HAVE FELT MORE GRATEFUL FOR THIS WEEK

DAY   MONTH   YEAR

THREE THINGS I'M GRATEFUL FOR

I GIVE TODAY A

SOMETHING I WANT TO REMEMBER ABOUT TODAY

SOMETHING I COULD HAVE BEEN MORE GRATEFUL FOR TODAY

MY INTENTION FOR
TOMORROW

DAY 352

DAY   MONTH   YEAR

THREE THINGS I'M GRATEFUL FOR

SOMETHING I WANT TO REMEMBER ABOUT TODAY

I GIVE TODAY A

MY INTENTION FOR TOMORROW

SOMETHING I COULD HAVE BEEN MORE GRATEFUL FOR TODAY

DAY   MONTH   YEAR

THREE THINGS I'M GRATEFUL FOR

I GIVE TODAY A

SOMETHING I WANT TO REMEMBER ABOUT TODAY

SOMETHING I COULD HAVE BEEN MORE GRATEFUL FOR TODAY

MY INTENTION FOR
TOMORROW

DAY   MONTH   YEAR

THREE THINGS I'M GRATEFUL FOR

SOMETHING I WANT TO REMEMBER ABOUT TODAY   I GIVE TODAY A

MY INTENTION FOR
TOMORROW

SOMETHING I COULD HAVE BEEN MORE GRATEFUL FOR TODAY

DAY   MONTH   YEAR

THREE THINGS I'M GRATEFUL FOR

I GIVE TODAY A

SOMETHING I WANT TO REMEMBER ABOUT TODAY

SOMETHING I COULD HAVE BEEN MORE GRATEFUL FOR TODAY

MY INTENTION FOR
TOMORROW

DAY 356

DAY   MONTH   YEAR

THREE THINGS I'M GRATEFUL FOR

SOMETHING I WANT TO REMEMBER ABOUT TODAY   I GIVE TODAY A

MY INTENTION FOR
TOMORROW   SOMETHING I COULD HAVE BEEN MORE GRATEFUL FOR TODAY

DAY 357

DAY   MONTH   YEAR

THREE THINGS I'M GRATEFUL FOR

I GIVE TODAY A

SOMETHING I WANT TO REMEMBER ABOUT TODAY

SOMETHING I COULD HAVE BEEN MORE GRATEFUL FOR TODAY

MY INTENTION FOR TOMORROW

GRATITUDE AND ATTITUDE ARE NOT CHALLENGES;
THEY ARE CHOICES.

ROBERT BRAATHE

SOMETHING I COULD HAVE BEEN MORE GRATEFUL FOR THIS WEEK

I GIVE THIS WEEK A

SOMETHING I WANT TO REMEMBER ABOUT THIS WEEK

MY INTENTION FOR NEXT
WEEK

SOMEONE I COULD HAVE FELT MORE GRATEFUL FOR THIS WEEK

DAY 358

DAY   MONTH   YEAR

THREE THINGS I'M GRATEFUL FOR

I GIVE TODAY A

SOMETHING I WANT TO REMEMBER ABOUT TODAY

SOMETHING I COULD HAVE BEEN MORE GRATEFUL FOR TODAY

MY INTENTION FOR
TOMORROW

DAY 359

THREE THINGS I'M GRATEFUL FOR

SOMETHING I WANT TO REMEMBER ABOUT TODAY

I GIVE TODAY A

MY INTENTION FOR
TOMORROW

SOMETHING I COULD HAVE BEEN MORE GRATEFUL FOR TODAY

DAY 360

DAY   MONTH   YEAR

THREE THINGS I'M GRATEFUL FOR

I GIVE TODAY A   SOMETHING I WANT TO REMEMBER ABOUT TODAY

SOMETHING I COULD HAVE BEEN MORE GRATEFUL FOR TODAY   MY INTENTION FOR TOMORROW

DAY 361

DAY   MONTH   YEAR

THREE THINGS I'M GRATEFUL FOR

SOMETHING I WANT TO REMEMBER ABOUT TODAY   I GIVE TODAY A

MY INTENTION FOR TOMORROW   SOMETHING I COULD HAVE BEEN MORE GRATEFUL FOR TODAY

DAY 362

DAY   MONTH   YEAR

THREE THINGS I'M GRATEFUL FOR

I GIVE TODAY A

SOMETHING I WANT TO REMEMBER ABOUT TODAY

SOMETHING I COULD HAVE BEEN MORE GRATEFUL FOR TODAY

MY INTENTION FOR TOMORROW

DAY   MONTH   YEAR

THREE THINGS I'M GRATEFUL FOR

SOMETHING I WANT TO REMEMBER ABOUT TODAY   I GIVE TODAY A

MY INTENTION FOR TOMORROW   SOMETHING I COULD HAVE BEEN MORE GRATEFUL FOR TODAY

DAY 364

DAY   MONTH   YEAR

THREE THINGS I'M GRATEFUL FOR

I GIVE TODAY A

SOMETHING I WANT TO REMEMBER ABOUT TODAY

SOMETHING I COULD HAVE BEEN MORE GRATEFUL FOR TODAY

MY INTENTION FOR TOMORROW

DAY 364

GRATITUDE, LIKE FAITH, IS A MUSCLE. THE MORE YOU USE IT, THE STRONGER IT GROWS, AND THE MORE POWER YOU HAVE TO USE IT ON YOUR BEHALF. IF YOU DO NOT PRACTICE GRATEFULNESS, ITS BENEFACTION WILL GO UNNOTICED, AND YOUR CAPACITY TO DRAW ON ITS GIFTS WILL BE DIMINISHED. TO BE GRATEFUL IS TO FIND BLESSINGS IN EVERYTHING. THIS IS THE MOST POWERFUL ATTITUDE TO ADOPT, FOR THERE ARE BLESSINGS IN EVERYTHING.

ALAN COHEN

SOMETHING I COULD HAVE BEEN MORE GRATEFUL FOR THESE PAST FOUR WEEKS

I GIVE THE PAST FOUR WEEKS A

SOMETHING I WANT TO REMEMBER ABOUT THE PAST FOUR WEEKS

MY INTENTION FOR THE NEXT FOUR WEEKS

SOMEONE I COULD HAVE FELT MORE GRATEFUL FOR THESE PAST FOUR WEEKS

DAY 365

DAY   MONTH   YEAR

THREE THINGS I'M GRATEFUL FOR

I GIVE TODAY A

SOMETHING I WANT TO REMEMBER ABOUT TODAY

SOMETHING I COULD HAVE BEEN MORE GRATEFUL FOR TODAY

MY INTENTION FOR
TOMORROW

DAY   MONTH   YEAR

THREE THINGS I'M GRATEFUL FOR

SOMETHING I WANT TO REMEMBER ABOUT TODAY   I GIVE TODAY A

MY INTENTION FOR   SOMETHING I COULD HAVE BEEN MORE GRATEFUL FOR TODAY
TOMORROW

12 MONTHS

YOU'VE MADE IT THROUGH A YEAR OF GRATITUDE! LET'S DO A FINAL CHECK-IN AND SEE WHAT THE PAST THREE MONTHS HAVE BROUGHT YOU.

SOMETHING I WANT TO REMEMBER ABOUT THE PAST THREE MONTHS

LOOKING BACK OVER THE PAST THREE MONTHS, I AM MOST GRATEFUL FOR

THE BIGGEST LESSON I LEARNED OVER THE PAST THREE MONTHS

SOMEONE OR SOMETHING I COULD HAVE FELT MORE GRATEFUL FOR DURING THE PAST THREE MONTHS

I GIVE THE PAST THREE MONTHS A

WHAT HAVE I BEEN UNABLE TO FEEL
GRATEFUL FOR DURING THE PAST THREE
MONTHS? CAN I REFORMULATE THAT
THOUGHT ANYWAY?

I AM GRATEFUL......

WHEN LOOKING BACK ON HOW I'VE RATED
MY WEEKS THUS FAR, THE NUMBERS TELL ME

MY INTENTION FOR THE NEXT THREE MONTHS

WHO HAVE I BEEN UNABLE TO FEEL GRATEFUL FOR DURING THE PAST THREE MONTHS? CAN I
REFORMULATE THAT THOUGHT ANYWAY? I AM GRATEFUL......

IT GOES WITHOUT SAYING

that I would love to hear your story and how you got along.

If we aren't already in touch one way or the other, you can find me here:

MARIELLE@MSWORDSMITH.NL
MSWORDSMITH.NL
FACEBOOK.COM/MSWORDSMITH
INSTAGRAM.COM/MARIELLESSMITH

If you never want to miss an update about what I'm doing, you can sign up for my newsletter here:

MSWORDSMITH.NL/NEWSLETTER

I would also love for you to leave a review on Goodreads or where you purchased this book. Honest reviews are vital to our work being found and read.

WANT MORE?

The more grateful I am, the more beauty I see.

Mary Davis

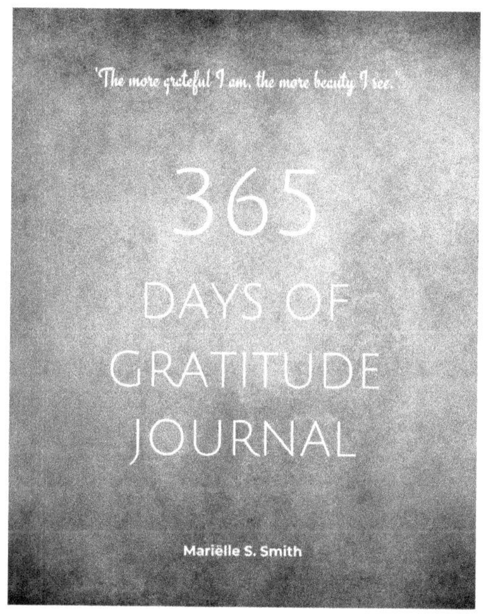

Volume 2 of the *365 Days of Gratitude Journal* comes out in autumn 2021.

Keep an eye on mswordsmith.nl/365daysofgratitude or sign up for my newsletter at mswordsmith.nl/newsletter to be the first to know when it's out.

ACKNOWLEDGEMENTS

I am immensely grateful that

ANDRI believes in everything I do

SHANE reintroduced me to the practice

MARTINE has mad Photoshop skills

and that my ARC team keeps providing me with the
best feedback and their endless support